AF386868

REQUIEM
—— FOR THE ——
REPUBLIC
CRITICAL ESSAYS

JAMES M BOURKE

authorHOUSE®

AuthorHouse™ UK
1663 Liberty Drive
Bloomington, IN 47403 USA
www.authorhouse.co.uk
Phone: UK TFN: 0800 0148641 (Toll Free inside the UK)
*   UK Local: 02036 956322 (+44 20 3695 6322 from outside the UK)*

Published by AuthorHouse 07/30/2021

ISBN: 978-1-6655-9185-0 (sc)
ISBN: 978-1-6655-9186-7 (e)

Print information available on the last page.

*Any people depicted in stock imagery provided by Getty Images are models,
and such images are being used for illustrative purposes only.
Certain stock imagery © Getty Images.*

This book is printed on acid-free paper.

CONTENTS

Rave on John Donne, rave on thy holy fool
Down through the weeks of ages
In the moss borne dark dank pools.
[Van Morrison, 1983]

GLOSSARY OF KEYWORDS

In my essays I am assuming that that many readers are familiar with such terms as liberalism, neoliberalism, secularism, humanism and scientism. However, since they are all much abused terms and overlap to some extent, I have compiled a short glossary of keywords relating to socio-political thinking in the 'New Ireland' and the cultural lexicon of liberalism.

abortion: The intentional expulsion of a human embryo or foetus from the uterus before it is viable. The word is derived from the Latin 'abortio' meaning 'miscarry'. Its first known use is c.1537. It was previously known as foeticide (1823) and criminal abortion (1899).

agnosticism: The belief that nothing is known or can be known of the existence or nature of God. (Oxford Dictionary of English, 2 ed. 2005. p.31) Thomas H. Huxley (1869) coined the word 'agnostic' which derives from the Greek 'ágnōstos' which means 'unknown or unknowable'.

atheism: The belief that God does not exist and that people of faith are 'irrational'. The most curious aspect of atheism is the absolute assertion of its adherents that their belief system is right and that all other belief systems are wrong.

Counter-culture: A way of life and a set of attitudes opposed to or at variance with the prevailing social norm. (Oxford Dictionary of English, 2nd ed. 2005, p. 395) culture: The abstract, learned, shared rules or norms for generating and governing behaviour and understanding experience. It covers a wide spectrum of attitudes towards such values as diversity, identity, tolerance, peace, respect, social cohesion, legacy issues, belief systems, religion and rituals, world view, native language, the environment, sustainable development. In anthropology, it includes material culture and oral culture.

humanism: A system of thought which places human interests and the mind of man above everything else exclusive of any supernatural dimension. (J. O'Donnell, 2005. Wordgloss: A Cultural Lexicon. p.41) The basic tenet of humanism is that human needs and values are more important than religious beliefs and consequently every person is free to create their own set of ethics. In 2005, Pope Benedict XV1 correctly announced that the greatest threat facing people of faith was a 'worldwide dictatorship of seemingly humanistic ideologies.'

language abuse: Language changes over time. However, language abuse refers to the deliberate distortion of word meaning for ideological or cultural reasons so that black means white and big means small. In 'Alice Through the Looking Glass' (1871) Humpty Dumpty says: 'When I use a word...it means just what I choose it to mean.' A similar viewpoint is evident in modern political discourse, journalism and the cultural lexicon of 'liberals'. For instance, many Irish politicians excel at euphemism, which is the art of lying. We are living in a post-truth society where fake news, government spin and political soundbites are the norm. For instance, the phrase 'abortion care' is widely used by abortionists to refer to the intentional killing of unborn life.

liberalism: Classical liberalism of the 19th century was a political and moral ideology based on liberty, consent of the governed (i.e. representative democracy), equality before the law and free and fair elections. Its core value was equality of esteem and entitlement regardless of race, religion, gender, ethnicity, income or social status. Its goal was to improve society by social justice, gradual social progress, civil liberties, reform of the law, protecting individual freedom, freedom of speech, freedom of assembly, freedom of peaceful protest, freedom of conscience and freedom of religion. However, modern liberalism, also known as social liberalism, is a very different matter. It is a woke form of liberalism, the very opposite of classical liberalism. It is a caricature of itself. It is driven by secularism, humanism and in some cases by socialism. It is the ideology of the 'New Ireland'. It is so bound up with secularism that two terms have become synonymous. At one time, it was cool to be liberal, but in modern usage it has become a pejorative term for tolerance of evil practices, such as abortion, infanticide, euthanasia, gay marriage, blasphemy and cultural indoctrination.

neoliberalism: Neoliberalism is a modern form of the classical economics of the 18th and 19th century. It is free-market capitalism tending to favour minimal government intervention in the economy, deregulation of markets, free trade, monetarism, the privatisation and underfunding of public services and a shift away from the Welfare State. It is firmly committed to globalisation. It is a utopian ideology concentrating on wealth, power and the economics of inequality. In the 1970s, it replaced Keynesian economic theory and was popularised in the USA by Milton Friedman of the Chicago School of Economic, endorsed by President Reagan in the US and Margaret Thatcher in the UK. It was imposed on most western economies by the IMF, the World Bank and the World Trade Organisation. However, it is no longer seen as an ideal economic system but rather as the root of the economic chaos which led to the financial meltdown of 2007-8.

political correctness (pc): The avoidance of any form of expression or action which is deemed offensive to other members of society and especially to people who are socially or physically disadvantaged. That is all very commendable except that it excludes those whose ideology is not the approved secularist version. For instance, it refers to people of faith as irrational. In former times, politeness and respect for others were ingrained in the Irish psyche. Those traits were called 'good manners'. In essence, political correctness (pc) is a weapon designed to silence people whose arguments cannot be refuted.

populism: The concept of populism differs from one political stance to another but in essence it refers to holding on to power by members of parliament who present themselves as 'the voice of the people'. They see themselves on the side of the common people rather than 'the elite' and they always speak of socio-political reforms and progressive policies, looking after the marginalised, especially manual workers, owners of small businesses and small farms. A good example is President Biden who tends to begin his speeches with the phrase: 'We, the people…' Of course, we know that he speaks only for the liberal / left in the USA.

secularism: Secularism is the most salient characteristic of modern liberalism. It is a political and social ideology that rejects all forms of religious faith and worship and the whole concept of metaphysical reality. It regards religion (and especially Christianity and Islam) as pernicious and it seeks to have all religion removed from civil policy - health, education and social welfare. It is more dangerous and deadly than the Covid-19 virus for the following reasons:

- It corrupts the minds of people.
- It rejects metaphysical reality, i.e. the supernatural.
- It promotes division, confusion and inequality.
- It demonises people of faith.
- It seeks to defund institutions under religious patronage, e.g. faith schools.

- It shows utter contempt for fundamental human rights, e.g. the right to life.
- It permits and promotes immoral practices e.g. blasphemy.

Secularists are full of missionary zeal and have the full backing of the media. Ireland has taken to secularism like a duck to water. Concepts such as moral responsibility, decency, honest dealing and clean living are deemed old-fashioned as are good manners, social etiquette, respect for the environment and pride in one's nation and one's traditional way of life. Ireland has become a vulgar nation, well on its way in the race to the bottom. Secularists are noted for the two of the worst and most demeaning human characteristics - ignorance and arrogance. They are utterly doctrinaire. They can see only their side of the road like the one-eyed Cyclops. The one thing they hate most of all is rational argument.

scientism: Some modern scientists regard themselves as superior to all other men and women. They try to extend scientific ideas and methods to matters of human, social and political concerns. They believe that there is nothing more to the mind of man than the physical motions and laws discovered by science. They believe that science is the only source of real knowledge (epistemology). Scientism is essentially excessive belief in the power of scientific knowledge. For some scientists, all knowledge is acquired by the 'scientific method' which consists in systematic observation, measurement, experiment and the formulation and testing of hypotheses. Science is wonderful; scientism is false.

The Great Reset: This term refers to the global reset of the world economy and the 'new norms' of modern society. It is a multi-faceted ideology embracing socialism, liberalism, secularism and modernism. It is directed by the World Economic Forum, which was founded by Klaus Schwab in 1971. It aims to create a new socialist world where individuals will own nothing, but will be happy! It is the brainchild of wealthy sociopaths acting out of self-interest. See essay 7 for more on the topic. Also see Time Magazine (30 October, 2020) which devotes a whole issue to The Great Reset.

Other terms that arise in the essays are explained either within the text or in endnotes.

INTRODUCTION

Requiem for the Republic is a collection of critical essays on the current state of the Republic of Ireland. They are an obituary for a republic that was born in blood, struggled to exist for a few years but never became a true republic. Since we are now celebrating a hundred years of nationhood, it seems that we have little to celebrate. The high republican ideals and goals of the founding fathers of the republic died with them. We are now living in a sham republic that has lost its soul, its national sovereignty and its moral principles. You may not agree, of course and you are entitled to your viewpoint. I am speaking as an alien in the 'New Ireland' which for me is the very antithesis of a true republic.

In my essays, I speak with frankness about members of the political elite in the Oireachtas (the Irish parliament) that have lost their reason and all moral compass. Sadly, many people do not seem to notice how the Republic, which was founded on Christian principles, is being transformed into a godless liberal/secularist state. My essays are a requiem for a republic that struggled to exist for three years (1916-1919) and subsequently withered over decades of national paralysis, culminating in the current sham republic that is known as the 'New Ireland'.

Having lived and worked overseas for forty years in the rump of the British Empire, I returned to Ireland in 2010. I soon discovered that Ireland was no longer the green and pleasant land that that I had left in the 80s. It had changed utterly but I had not changed at all. Hence, I am now an alien in my homeland. In my novel 'Confessions of an Alien' (2016) the main character says: 'My world has collapsed, my ship has sunk and I have ended up as flotsam on the shore. There is darkness in my soul. I do not belong.' Those words sum up my dilemma.

As an alien and an outsider, I can perhaps see things more objectively than people who have never been abroad. I see clearly some things that many people have chosen not to see. An alien has no agenda, no fear and no political affiliation. As an alien, I have a keen eye for noticing falsity, human frailty, socio-political ideology and endemic corruption. My problem is that I cannot lie, which is a distinct disadvantage in a post-truth society. I see a government driven by abuse of power, self-interest, secularism, corruption and falsity. I see a government that has legalised human killing, blasphemy, the economics of inequality and blatant discrimination. It seems to me that the so-called 'New Ireland' is a Kafkaesque state, a nation that has become dishonest with itself.

The essays are my personal reflections and, being an alien, I can speak frankly. I know that my views on the state of the nation are contestable and will be contested. My comments and criticisms relate almost entirely to the galloping secularism which the government, the media and various state-funded bodies are promoting with evangelical zeal. I do not question the competence and integrity of the great majority of Irish TDs and Senators but as in Hitler's republic, there are always poisonous snakes lurking in the long grass. I refer to them as 'little pharaohs' and they tend to reside in the Departments of Health, Education, Social Welfare and Children. One thing is clear; we have come to the end of an era. The old Ireland is dead. Common decency, truth and good manners no longer exist in the 'New Ireland'. The new norms are intolerance, falsity and yob culture.

The national emblem of Ireland is the harp whose ethereal and captivating music was deemed to reflect the harmony, joy and purity of the Irish nation. However, that was long ago. The harp is now silent and the Celtic Christian nation it represented is now dead. The Republic that it once proudly celebrated is no more - a theme expressed in the Thomas Moore melody, 'The Harp that Once':

The harp that once through Tara's halls
The soul of music shed
Now hangs as mute on Tara's walls
As if that soul were fled.

It is hardly necessary for me to add that my essays are my reflections, my opinion and my observations. They are liberally sprinkled with personal markers such as 'it seems to me', 'it appears that', 'from my perspective' etc. which clearly indicate my viewpoint on specific topics. Any facts mentioned are referenced by source, either in the text or in endnotes. As a writer, I have to speak the truth as I know it. For me, truth matters above all else. My essays are essentially about truth versus lies. We are living in a post-truth era. Our government lies. Our politicians lie. Our media lies. When a lie is repeated, it is often accepted as true. People believe a lie when they want it to be true.

My essays deal specifically with the Republic of Ireland but they also reflect the current global cultural conflict that exists between two diametrically opposed ideologies, namely, Christian conservative values and the new norms of the modern 'liberal' state. My essays are a battle cry for a more just republic, for traditional values, for the pro-life cause and for an end to corruption in the Church and in society. Nothing I say is new or contentious. I am simply repeating the teaching of the Gospel – a teaching that the modern 'liberal' world does not like to hear. My essays are a searing indictment of the falsity and toxic agenda of the modern so-called 'liberal' state.

James M Bourke
20ˢᵗ July, 2021.

1

THE IDEA OF A REPUBLIC

In this essay, my thesis is that the Republic of Ireland is not a true republic; it has become a sham republic, a republic in name only. First, it is necessary to define the term 'republic' and to discuss the characteristics of a true republic.

Republic defined:

The Oxford Dictionary of English (2005) defines a republic as 'a state in which supreme power is held by the people and their elected representatives'. Two fundamental attributes of a republic are (a) representative democracy and (b) the absence of a centralised ruling elite. Any state that calls itself a republic must embody the two complementary notions of the right of citizens to participate in government and freedom from the arbitrary rule of despots. The term 'republic' derives from the Latin 'res' (concerns) and 'publicus'(of the people). In ancient Athens and later in Rome, the idea of a republic was based on certain values or 'virtues' such as equality, justice, truth, the common good, freedom and fundamental human rights. The core characteristic of a republic is representative democracy which is best defined in the Gettysburg Address (1863) as 'government of the people, by the people, for the people'. Representative democracy is bottom up, not top down. It is founded on upward control and shaped by the common people. Furthermore, a republic, just like every other form of parliamentary democracy, will insist on national sovereignty. It must have the power to make its own laws, protect is own borders and decide what is best in its national interest.

The word 'republic' is a much abused term. Many despotic regimes call themselves a republic, for instance, the Central African Republic or the Peoples Republic of China or Castro's Cuba. Nearer home, Cromwell was the first Republican in Britain. However, his republic did not last long. It was a dictatorship just as pernicious as that of the Stuart monarchy that came before and after it.

Judged by the criteria outlined above, the Republic of Ireland cannot be called a true republic. It fails the test of representative democracy. It fails the test of freedom from the arbitrary rule of a self-serving elite. And it fails the test of national sovereignty. I am not saying that the Republic is ruled by a despotic regime but I am saying that it is ruled by a political elite which seeks to transform a Christian country into a godless secularist state. The true meaning of the word 'republic' takes us back to Plato and Cicero.

Plato's Republic:

Plato's seminal work 'The Republic' (375) B.C[1] describes the ideal republic – the just state and the just society. Written in ten books, in the form of Socratic dialogues, it is a philosopher's response to the ills plaguing the ancient Athenian state. For Plato, the ideal republic has to be founded on four 'virtues' – wisdom, courage, moderation and justice. The ideal rulers are wise men (never women!), in other words, philosophers. In Book 6, he refers to the 'ship of fools' – a metaphor for a dysfunctional government that many writers have cited in recent times. Plato had grave reservations about Athenian democracy. He states that in a democracy, the people rule but they are not experts, i.e. wise men. Hence, in his view, democracy is irrational. We have to remember that Plato's ideas are abstract entities or 'universals' which are contrasted with their objects or 'particulars' in the material world.

Cicero's Republic:

During a time of political corruption and violence in Rome, Cicero[2] delivered many famous orations on what he deemed the ideal form of government. He also wrote two famous books on the subject, 'De Re Publica' and 'De Legibus'.[3] The Roman Republic was 400 years old when Cicero was elected to the Senate in 74 B.C. The Senate was the centre of power. It set government policies and debated proposed laws which had to be ratified by 12 tribunes chosen by the plebians to protect their interests. However, by Cicero's time, in spite of elaborate checks and balances, bribery, extortion and the vested interests of the old patrician families had undermined the system.

In 'De Legibus' Cicero expounds the principle of Natural Law which he asserts is the cornerstone of all jurisprudence. He says that all law 'is implanted in Nature, which commands what ought to be done and forbids the opposite.'[4] Furthermore, he asserts that Natural Law is eternal, unchangeable and binding at all times on all people. Hence, the Constitution has to be in harmony with Natural Law in order to achieve justice and fairness in a society riven by the conflicting interests and demands of the patricians (the Senate) and the plebians (the common people).

The 'evil' empires:

The Roman Republic ended in 27 B.C with the establishment of the Roman Empire which gradually spread its wings across most of Europe, including Britain, the Middle East and North Africa. The Roman Empire finally ended in 476 A.D. The story of its decline and fall is told by

Edward Gibbon (1872).[5] At school, we learned about the rise and fall of the anciens régimes – the Byzantine Empire (280- 1460 A.D.), the Holy Roman Empire (800 – 1806), the Ottoman Empire (1299 – 1923 A.D), the Prussian Empire (1525 – 1918), the British Empire (1600 -1997), the Russian Empire (1721 – 1917), the French Empire (1804 – 1870) and the Austro-Hungarian Empire (1867 – 1918). Then in the early years of the 20th century, many of the colonised nations began rattling the gates of the great empires. The Great War (1914 – 1918) was a clash of the old empires. On one side were the combined Central Powers and on the other were the Western Allies. However, the real issue was the clash between the declining great powers and the emerging nation states of Europe. Europe was ripe for re-making in 1914. Everyone knew how the war started but few understood what it was about. At that time, the Irish Parliamentary Party at Westminster had won Home Rule for Ireland but it was put on hold when the Great War broke out. Its leader, John Redmond went to great lengths in persuading Irishmen to rally to the cause of defending Europe against the Hun. Some 201,000 Irishmen served under the British flag and 35,000 perished on the bloody battlefields of the Great War. Of course, the generals did not tell the troops that they were mere cannon fodder in a great imperial chess game. They were told that they were fighting 'for King and Country'. They were told that the 'Prussian militarism' i.e. Germany, was about to pounce on their territory and that they had a moral duty to defend the homeland and the small nations of Europe.

A 'terrible beauty' is born:

The Great War changed everything in Ireland, which was one of the small European states seeking independence from its powerful neighbour and when Irish rebels staged an uprising in 1916 it was suppressed with unspeakable savagery by the British Army. However, that act of callous brutality aroused enormous national anger and turned the nation against the old enemy. The 'terrible beauty' that W. B. Yeats wrote about was crushed. However, Irish men and women took up arms and declared independence at the first meeting of the first Dáil at the Mansion House in Dublin on 21st January 1919. For the second time, Ireland was declared a republic at that meeting. However, the old empire was determined to hold on to its oldest colony. Dublin was the second capital of the Empire and if some misguided freedom-fighters in Dublin tried to break free, the empire would strike back, fearing the ripple effect that secession would cause across the Great British Empire on which the sun never set. Britain declared war on the nascent republic and a bitter 'war of the running dogs' ensued, which lasted two and half years, from 21st January 1919 to 11th July 1921. Then, with both sides unable to win an outright victory, a settlement called the Anglo-Irish Treaty was agreed. Most of Ireland (26 of the 32 counties) was declared a Free State i.e. no longer within the British Empire but it was not a republic and it had to concede six of the Northern counties to the United Kingdom. The Anglo-Irish Treaty was signed in London on 6th December 1921 and was ratified by the Dáil on 7th January, 1922. It was a close call, 64 votes for and 57 against and, as often happens in such situations, it led to the civil war which went on from June 1922 to May 1923. It was not until 1949 that Ireland formally became a republic, following the passage of the Republic of Ireland Act in November, 1948. However, it was a fractured republic and the old 'Irish Question' remained unanswered.

Joining the European Union:

Following the Battle of Kinsale in 1601, the whole country was conquered by the English Crown and for 320 years the Irish fought against the occupier to regain their independence. Then having finally won independence in 1921, some 50 years later it surrendered its sovereignty to a foreign power - the European Union, (the EEC, as it was known then). The nation was divided on the issue and tried to leave the EU in June 2008 by rejecting the Treaty of Lisbon in a referendum. However, the government insisted on a re-run of the referendum in October 2009 and persuaded the electorate to change their mind. My view, which is not shared by many, is that joining the EU was a mistake for the simple reason that direct democracy from Brussels does not and cannot function uniformly across the EU. Moreover, national sovereignty is a key component of a true republic. In any case, Ireland was always part of Europe and its people were always European in outlook and culture. They did not become more European by joining the European Union. What Irish people did not seem to notice was that the EU wants to become a military power. It is possible, therefore, that under the principle of 'harmonisation', the Republic will one day be obliged to surrender its neutrality, having already surrendered its sovereignty.

What a republic is not:

In conclusion, it seem obvious to me that the Republic of Ireland is not, and probably never was, a true republic for the following reasons:

- A real republic does not surrender its sovereignty to a foreign power.
- A real republic is not dictated to by a ruling elite in a national parliament nor does it take dictation and direction for 'little pharaohs' in its various Departments.
- A real republic does not engage in vile propaganda, brainwashing, misinformation, euphemism and outright lies.
- A real republic does not tear up the Constitution which enshrines the fundamental rights and entitlements of its citizens.
- A real republic does not legalise human killing at the beginning or the end of life.

- A real republic does not subvert the traditional culture, values, beliefs and ethos of its citizens.
- A real republic does not legalise human killing, blasphemy, same-sex marriage and sexual practices against the order of nature.
- A real republic does not punish its marginalised citizens by pushing them into poverty, austerity, homelessness and misery.
- A real republic does not fail to provide a free and efficient national health service for all its citizens as well as proper mental health and home health services.
- A real republic does not ride roughshod over the civil liberties and freedom of conscience of its citizens.

I am saying that the past and present governments of the Republic are characterised by some or all of the above attributes and hence the state has ceased to be a true republic. I am saying that Irish politicians would do well to remember the words of the founding fathers of the Republic in the document called 'The Proclamation of the Republic (Easter 1916). I am saying that the Irish Republic was founded on an idea. If we do not preserve and honour that idea, we have nothing. If we destroy the ethical foundation of the state, we are no longer a true republic. In the essays that follow, I shall provide ample evidence to support my thesis.

Endnotes:

1   Benjamin Jowett (2016). 'The Republic: An English Translation'. Available online at www.gutenberg.org/files/55201/55201h/55201-htm Retrieved 28.10.2020.

2   Marcus Tullius Cicero (106 – 43 B.C) has been resurrected in recent times by Robert Harris's gripping books 'The Cicero Trilogy'. In fact, his ideas never went away. He was a famous orator, lawyer, consul, senator and philosopher. The Roman Republic was 400 years old when he was elected to the Senate, a very corrupt body in ancient Rome – 'a city of glory built on a river of filth.' In former times, his orations (in Latin) were required reading for the Matriculation

Examination in Ireland. His two books, 'De Re Publica' and 'De Legibus' deal with his views on the ideal form of government and the principle of Natural Law. He was assassinated in 43 B.C. on the orders of Mark Antony.

3   Clinton Walker Keyes (1988). 'De Re Publica; De Legibus'. (Text in Latin and English). Harvard University Press.

4   Keyes op. cit. De Legibus, Book 3, p.62

5   Edward Gibbon (1872). 'The Decline and Fall of the Roman Empire'. Available online at www.gutenberg.org/files/25717/25717-htm Retrieved 30.10.202

2

FROM FREE STATE TO SECULARIST STATE

My thesis, as stated in Essay 1, is that the current Republic of Ireland is not a true republic. It is a pretend republic. It does not have the defining attributes of a real republic which were discussed in Essay 1. However, our politicians have managed to create the illusion that the former Free State is now an authentic democratic republic whereas, in fact, it is a mere shadow of a true republic. The Irish Free State and the so-called Independent Ireland which followed it, failed to uphold the lofty ideals of the founding fathers of the Republic It is true that the Republic is a parliamentary democracy. It is true that Irish people have free and fair elections to the Dáil and to local authorities but not to the Senate. There is no evidence of vote rigging. However, the question at issue here is whether it is a true republic. In order to answer that question, we have to apply two tests regarding (a) national sovereignty and (b) popular sovereignty i.e. representative democracy. My contention is that the Republic of Ireland fails both of these tests. It was a republic for six days in 1916 but in following years the high ideals of republicanism withered due to the political bitterness over the Treaty that created the Irish Free State in December 1921 and January 1922. We do not even know for sure when the State became a republic. There are three possible answers to that puzzle, each partly right and partly wrong. Some historians say that we became a republic in 1916 with the Proclamation of

9

the Republic on Easter Sunday 1916. However, the Rising lasted only six days and all the signatories of the Proclamation were court-martialled and shot. Did the Republic die with them? Is seems that it did not. In fact the horrific execution of the 1916 patriots only fuelled the fire of freedom and Arthur Griffith's Sinn Féin party romped to victory in General Election in December 1918, after which it convened the first Dáil in January 1919 at which it ratified the Republic that had been proclaimed in 1916. So was that the date on which the Republic was born? Some historian say it was and others disagree, pointing out that the British declared war on the new Republic which went on sporadically for two and half years from January 1919 to July 1921 after which the 1919 Republic was disestablished by the Anglo-Irish Treaty which the Irish government signed in December 1921 and had it ratified in the Dáil in January 1922. Was the Free State a republic? Clearly, it was not. It was a half-formed political entity with Dominion status. A bloody civil war followed which left the country divided and embittered for generations. It was many years later that the Republic was formally proclaimed by the passing of the Republic of Ireland Act 1948, which came into force in 1949. Hence, the Republic is 72 years old. We are currently celebrating the centenary of Independence as agreed in 1921/1922. However, an independent Free State is not a republic. National sovereignty is a key constituent of a republic. The partition of Ireland was seen in 1921/1922 as a temporary arrangement but we know now that there is nothing more permanent than a 'temporary arrangement.'

In order to understand the background to the struggle for Irish freedom and self-government, we have to know how something of the long history of Ireland as a British colony. I shall not dwell on the four centuries of of British rule (or misrule) on the island of Ireland. While on a lecture tour in the USA in 1931, W. B. Yeats spoke of 'Four Bells – four deep tragic notes in Irish history.'

The first bell was the Flight of the Earls in 1607 A.D. following the Nine Years' War (1594-1603). That event was a watershed in Irish history, marking the end of old Gaelic world and the onset of the systematic suppression of national Gaelic identity, culture, language, religion, customs and traditions.

The second bell was the Battle of the Boyne on 12 July 1690, when the Protestant King William of Orange beat the Catholic army under the exiled King James 11. That event marked the consolidation of the Protestant Ascendancy in Ireland and it is still celebrated with pride by the Orange Order and the Loyalist population of Northern Ireland. The 18th century was the Age of Enlightenment in Europe but it was a time of great hardship for the landless peasants of Ireland as noted by Goldsmith in his poem 'The Deserted Village'.

The third bell was the coming of revolutionary influence from France following the French Revolution which inspired the United Irishmen to create an independent Irish Republic. But it all ended in failure after Wolfe Tone's ships failed to land at Bantry Bay in 1796 and the United Ireland rebels were defeated at the Battle of Vinegar Hill in 1798.

The fourth bell Yeats describes as 'the beginning of our age' following the death of Parnell, the death of Home Rule, the turning away from parliamentary democracy, the rise of Fenian movement and the birth of 'the terrible beauty' (the Irish Republic) at Easter 1916. In the years following the Great War, the map of Europe changed dramatically as nation-states freed themselves from the hegemony of the old empires. The British Empire reluctantly had to allow some its colonies to secede, Ireland being the first. However, the British were never good at borders, not only in Ireland but also in the Middle East, Southeast Asia and Africa. Irish independence came at a price. Part of the country had to remain a British colony.

Yeats's synoptic history of the four centuries of British rule in Ireland is very sketchy and surprisingly makes no mention of the Great Famine but it is interesting in that it comes from a man raised the in Protestant Anglo-Irish tradition. In fact, many of the Irish patriots were Protestants – Parnell,

Wolfe Tone, Robert Emmet and Constance Markievicz. The Catholic hierarchy was for most part anti-republican. During the civil war (June 1922 to May 1923) those on the republican (anti-Treaty) side were excommunicated!

The Free State struggled to convert independence into a better quality of life for its citizens. There was no economic boom, only doom, gloom and massive unemployment. Irish families faced years of austerity. Many writers have described the grinding poverty of those lean years and the enormous task facing the Free State government in building a productive economy and national infrastructure – power stations, hospitals, housing and slum clearance. Eamon de Valera was the dominant figure in those early years of the Free State. He was a staunch republican and an astute politician. As a survivor of the 1916 Rising, he was held in high esteem and much admired for his intransigence on the 'Irish Question'. In 1937, he had the Free State Constitution re-written and ratified by the Dáil. In it, sweeping changes were made. It asserted that the national territory was the whole island of Ireland. It also recognised the special position of the Catholic Church. Irish was declared the national language. Those provisions naturally did not amuse the British government and obviously alienated Ulster Unionists. De Valera was a man of unbending integrity which is rare in politicians. He and his Fianna Fáil party restored national pride by gradually revoking several of the provisions of the Anglo-Irish Treaty. He abolished the Oath of Allegiance to the British monarch and the land-purchase annuities. Britain retaliated by imposing a 20% tariff on Irish imports and the Free State responded in like manner. The 'economic war' continued up to 1938. De Valera's standing was greatly enhanced by boldly defending the country's neutrality during the World War 2, a stance that enraged Churchill. His successor, Sean Lemass, was also, like de Valera, a staunch Republican, a veteran of the Easter Rising 1916 and the War of Independence. However, seeing that the country was becoming an economic wasteland, he set about developing industry and opening up the Irish economy and thus set the country on a strong economic footing which continued after his retirement in 1966. The country had regained its self-confidence and for the first time Ireland's voice was heard on the world stage, in the UN and its many agencies worldwide.

The counter-culture movement:

Sociologists tell us that the world changed in the 60s with the coming of the counter-culture movement heralded by pop music, hippies, Flower power, anti-war protest, free love and smoking cannabis. By the mid-seventies, Irish culture, like that in Britain, had changed utterly and found its voice in the underground magazine 'Hot Press'.[1] The 'ballroom of romance' culture had given way to rock and roll and the pursuit of pleasure, raves and anti-social behaviour. In 1979, heroin hit the streets of Dublin. It is probably true to say that ever since then the Republic has been on a downward spiral intellectually, morally and culturally. It also became more liberal, more secularist and more anti-Catholic. New norms were established by counter-culture, the rise of gay and feminist activism while the Catholic Church retreated into silence due to its sordid clerical sex abuse scandals. At the same time, the country became more prosperous. Then in 1973 the Republic joined the EEC which boosted the Irish economy a great deal. However, it seems extraordinary that a country which had resisted foreign occupation for over 400 years should suddenly and gladly surrender national sovereignty to a foreign power – the EEC (now the EU) in Brussels. The surrender of national sovereignty was, in my view, the last nail in the coffin of the republic. Ireland can no longer claim to be an independent republic; it is a colony of the European Union. I know that most people will disagree with me and say that national sovereignty is an obsolete notion. My point is that Ireland was always European in outlook and culture. We did not become more European by joining the EU. We simply reverted to colonial status.

The democratic deficit:

In the past, many famous Irish men and women insisted that a real republic must be based on representative democracy; it must speak the truth, defend human rights and uphold moral values and Ireland's unique cultural heritage. They insisted on national sovereignty and popular sovereignty. We had great thinkers, writers and politicians in former times, for instance Henry Grattan, Daniel O'Connell, Charles Stewart Parnell, Edmund Burke, Patrick Pearse and more recently John Hume and poet Seamus Heaney. Sadly, they have all gone now and we are left with politicians who lack moral courage, academics who lack intellectual honesty and a toxic media dominated by secularist and feminist ideology. The Irish government has legalised human killing, blasphemy and same-sex marriage. It bends the knee to neoliberalism and the economy of inequality. It seems to me that certain members of the inner circle, i.e. the cabinet, are acting like 'little pharaohs' while backbenchers sit on their hands since they are whipped into conformity and have become in effect nodding donkeys. A few brave men and women still speak the truth but they are despised and denounced by the media. In the 'New Ireland' speaking the truth has gone out of fashion. For instance, the writer and journalist John Waters[2] was forced to resign from The Irish Times in 2014 for daring to speak the truth about the 'New Ireland.'

We should have learned from history that it is always unwise to give absolute power to a central government whose members' top priority is remaining in power by hook or by crook. The essential characteristic of good government is representative democracy, in other words popular sovereignty, the voice of the people. A parliamentary system of government is not democratic unless it is represents the concerns, wishes and views of the people. Irish people at not very good at 'noticing'. They often fail to notice the ideological position of the candidates that they vote for in an election. They do not seem to know that politicians seeking election to the

Dáil or the local County Council are often two-faced. For instance, before the general election in 2016, candidates selected by Fianna Fáil said they would never vote for abortion but when the Abortion Bill came before the Dáil in 2018 they voted for it.

Charles de Gaulle once said that politics is too important to be left to the politicians. A true republic needs wise men and women, people of integrity and to carry out the will of the people. We know what happens when the state is ruled by a 'ship of fools'. Sadly, the 'New Ireland' is no longer a republic. The ruling parties in the Oireachtas behave like 'little pharaohs' rather than representatives of the people. A good example of this is the Fine Gael party which drafted Abortion Bill (2018). Its leadership steadfastly refused to allow any amendments to its brutal terms, which gives any female over the age of 15 the right to terminate an unwanted pregnancy for any reason up to 12 weeks and on restrictive grounds thereafter. The former Minister for Health led the pack clamouring for abortion. Did he listen to the voice of the people? Of course, not. He listened only to the godfathers of abortion in the Oireachtas, to the pro-abortion media and to a raft of state-funded bodies under the control of rabid feminists. Irish people did not vote for the deliberate killing of 6,666 unwanted unborn babies each year much less for the intentional killing of any born baby that managed to survive a botched abortion. It was the Fine Gael government with the support of the great majority of member of parliament which legalised human killing. Only nine members of parliament voted against the Abortion Bill. I shall have more to say on the that matter in Essay 7.

On paper, the Republic is a parliamentary democracy but it has ceased to be a representative democracy. Today, it is more like a self-serving oligarchy. The 'few' now rule over the 'many' by means of devious mechanisms which are the very antithesis of a representative democracy. I am referring especially to bogus agencies such as the Citizens' Assembly which the government convenes to propose changes to the Constitution, making it more inclusive, more liberal and more secularist. Now a group of

99 individuals is selected to speak on behalf of the nation and to promote the government's agenda of galloping secularism. For example, in April 2021 the Citizens' Assembly was directed to review and amend Article 41 of the Constitution, which recognises the Family "as the natural primary and fundamental unit group of society" and as a "moral institution possessing certain inalienable and imprescriptible rights" which are "antecedent and superior to all positive law". In the 'New Ireland' of 2021 such language is anathema to our secularist government and must be removed from the Constitution. Furthermore, democracy is also subverted by lobbying by unelected bodies such as the Irish Family Planning Association, Amnesty International, the secular media, and 'advisers' to Ministers. All of those unelected persons and bodies represent a chilling threat to democracy in a real republic. Irish people do not seem the notice the cosy relationship that exists between members of the Oireachtas and financial institutions. They do not seem to notice the revolving door between government ministers and lobbyists in high finance. The classic example of this unholy relationship was the decision of the government to bail out the banks after the collapse of the Celtic Tiger in 2007/8 at a cost to the taxpayer of €65 billion.

At school we were told that a fish rots from the head down. I do not know whether that is true or not but I do know the a bad government rots from the centre. True democracy is bottom up, not top down. It is founded on representative democracy. We would do well to consider the social thought of Edmund Burke for whom the best life begins in the 'little platoons', namely, family, church and the local community. From one's local community one proceeds towards a love for one's borough or county, and thence to a love for one's country and thereafter to a love for mankind. He says: 'To be attached to the subdivision, to love the little platoons we belong to in society, is the first principle (the germ as it were) of public affections.'[3] Burke emphasises society over the state. He defends the culture and traditions of society, the moral order, the rule of law and the social contract. For him, popular consent is key. He reminds us that we all have a role to play in safeguarding our national identity, our native culture and traditions and our moral principles. He is not against change since all progress involves change but he distinguishes between positive and negative change. He most certainly would never have approved of the new norms that a secularist / liberal government seeks to impose on its citizens leading ultimately to a Stasi-esque State. I am sure that he would not want to live in the 'New Ireland' - in a secularist state that puts prejudice before principles, a state that seeks to impose its secularist ideology on people rooted in faith and traditional values, such as truth, honesty and parity of esteem for all.

The gospel of secularism:

The gospel of secularism is supposedly based on reason and science but they are the penumbra of a different ideology. I know what I am talking about. As a writer, I listen to people and I try to understand their viewpoint on various issues of importance. A lot of my informal conversations revolve around the 'New Ireland'. Most of the young people I happen to meet are devout secularists. They tell me that Irish society has 'moved on'. We now live in a new era of personal freedom, where 'I can be me'. In the 'New Ireland,' thinking people have rejected the notion of 'received morality' i.e. the Ten Commandments. In the modern world, people are free to make their own moral choices, to have fun, and break free from the chains of religion. They say that good living begins with individual choice. They are told that there are no absolutes in life, no universal principles. We are 'normal people' now. We have 'progressed'. We have killed God and liberated ourselves from the tyranny of religion and especially from the misogynistic and homophobic teaching of the Catholic Church. The old era of Catholic Ireland is dead. People of faith are regarded as irrational and modern Irish people today are the first generation of rational human beings on the planet. They have erased the past and all that 'republican gibberish' about national pride, Irish identity, Gaelic culture and Christian ideology. They have, at long last, walked away from the fairy tales and fables in the Bible. They are now living in the real world. Just look at our secular government's proud record in government. They have legalised divorce, abortion, same-sex marriage, blasphemy and objective sex education in all Primary and post-Primary schools. Irish people now share the liberal culture of progressive EU member states and they are happy to have turned their backs on the Christian republicanism that de Valera and his right-wing Catholic bigots imposed on the State in the 1937 Constitution. Fortunately, our government has torn up most of de Valera's Constitution and brought its provisions up to date to reflect the reality of life in the 21st century. In the 'New Ireland', the future is secular. Ireland's liberal ideology is equally embraced by right-wing neoliberals and left-wing socialists. People in the 'New Ireland' belong to a different era. They are now free at last and can do what they like.

Of course, you cannot argue rationally with devout secularists. They are utterly dogmatic and they keep repeating sound bites such as 'The future is secular.' They do not know that the Republic was always a secular state. It was never a theocratic state. The Irish Constitution enshrines the separation of powers. There is a world of difference between the words 'secular' and 'secularist'. When secularists speak or write, they use the cultural lexicon of the 'New Ireland.' They will not listen when I point out that they are wholly illiberal. They do not understand the meaning of the word 'liberal'. Modern 'liberal' politicians look after their own own and when it comes to allocating funding, they make sure that their members get a slice of the salami. Every liberal politician in Leinster House has one great ambition and that is to become a MEP - to make it to the ultimate gravy train, the EU Parliament.

I am happy to be an alien in the 'New Ireland'. I will have nothing to do with fake liberalism and political correctness. I do not belong. For me, truth matters. For me, integrity matters. For me, all life matters, not only

Black lives but every human life. I am of a different era and a different persuasion. I happen to believe that we must retain moral integrity to live in harmony in society where common goodness is its own reward and where we do not harm, much less kill, any other human life. I cannot subscribe to the toxic culture of human killing and woke secularism which masquerades under the umbrella of liberalism. However, it seems that only an alien can notice the sheer awfulness of the 'New Ireland.' The message I hear from government is that we have 'moved on' and 'we are all in this together'. Even church leaders are silent on the shocking moral stance of the 'New Ireland'. The toxic ideology of secularism is, like the deadly COVID virus, in the very air we breathe.

As I have outlined above, Ireland was occupied by a foreign power for 400 years and it was the first nation to secede from the British Empire. The Irish fili (poets) spoke in vitriolic terms of the rape of Róisín Dubh[4] by the Ugly Vulcan. Then Ireland became a Free State, even though it wanted to become an independent republic. Of course, Britain decided that is could not allow its oldest colony to secede from the Empire and declared war on the nascent self-proclaimed republic. The Irish fought back for two and half years and won token independence in 1921, a century ago. After a protracted guerrilla war, the two sides signed the Anglo-Irish Treaty. The most contentious clauses of the treaty were the partition of Ireland and the disestablishment of the Irish Republic which had been declared by the first Dáil in January 1919. The civil war which followed tore the heart out of the Free State and set a bitter legacy for the emerging Republic and for national unity. Eventually in 1948 the Republic was formally declared but it was no more than a hollow gesture. The Free State had become a dysfunctional State long before it became a dysfunctional Republic. Worse was to follow. Firstly, the ruling elite determined to make a cultural transition from the old Christian culture and the traditional values of the de Valera era to a liberal modern secularist State. From the 70s onwards, the new liberal / secularist State began to emerge and was fully endorsed by the servile media, by left-leaning academics, by populist writers and by the feminist and gay movements. And as a result, people of faith, have to live as best they can in a chaotic State, victims of secularist ideology and secularist syncretism. Secondly, in 1973, Irish people were persuaded to surrender national sovereignty to the EEC. Everyone seemed happy to be governed from Brussels by a liberal and secularist oligarchy. Hence, one more bell has to added to W. B. Yeats' four bells. The fifth and final bell refers to the transforming of the Christian nation-state into a 'liberal' secularist State on joining the European Union which is determined to extinguish the cultural heritage of each nation-state and to eradicate Europe's Christian ideology. The citizens of the New Europe and the New Ireland must turn their backs on their traditional Christian beliefs, culture and heritage. The old Christian states of Europe must be transformed into a modern secularist super-state. They must embrace the new secularist ideology of the liberal elite. However, the EU is already facing dismemberment. After months of negotiation, the UK has withdrawn from the EU. British people no longer want to be locked into rigid trade restrictions, social and immigration policies, red tape and stifling bureaucracy. Other states may follow Britain's example, in particular Poland, Hungary and Greece. By now, the EU leadership should have realized that one size does not fit all and that European nation-states will hold onto their cultural identity and Christian ideology.

Now, in 2021, we are celebrating a hundred years of nationhood but we should be chanting a requiem for a Republic that failed many of its citizens. A fitting requiem for the demise of the Republic is the short poem 'Mise Eire' which was composed by Padraic Pearce in1912. Translated into English, it reads:

<blockquote>
I am Ireland:
I am older than the Hag of Beara[6].
Great my glory:
I who bore Cuchulainn, the brave.
</blockquote>

Great my shame:

My own children that sold their mother.

I am Ireland,

Lonelier than the Hag of Beara.

Endnotes:

1   Hot Press: A music and politics magazine based in Dublin, first issued in 1977.

2   John Waters (2018). 'Give Us Back the Bad Roads'. Dublin: Currach Press.

3   Edmund Burke: 'Reflections on the Revolution in France', pp.136-137.

4   Róisín Dubh: 'Dark Rosaleen', a metaphor and poetic symbol for Irish nationalism

5   The Hag (Cailleach) of Beara is the Celtic goddess of winter. A massive rock facing the sea on the Beara Peninsula is said to be her fossilised remains. The Beara Peninsula lies between Kenmare and Bantry Bay.

3

ON SOCIAL CONTROL AND ABUSE OF POWER

In Ireland and across Europe, the terms liberal, neoliberal and secularist go together hand in hand to define the kind of governance that is known as 'liberal democracy'. It is not a new way of defining the relationship between the ruler and the ruled. It goes back to the 17th century in Europe. It is based on the notion of paternalistic duty on the part of the wise ruler towards the unruly rabble. The common people need to be controlled and inspired by the wisdom and prudence that comes from the elite values and norms of the ruling class. The great delusion of our time is that the ruling elite is fulfilling the wishes of the people. If you look at the facts on the ground, you will see that ruling elite will always rule out of self-interest, putting domination above consent, propaganda before truth, prejudice before principles, ideology before liberty, profit before people and 'dark money' before everything else. Good governance in the modern world can best be described as 'elective dictatorship'. It is the very opposite of representative democracy.

All philosophers from Plato to Ludwig Wittgenstein have agonised over good governance, a just society and ethics – the way we should live in the world. For instance, in the 17th century, Thomas Hobbes (1651) believed that all human action was motivated by self-interest, hence the idea of a just society was an illusion. Man was by nature pre-ordained to live a life of misery ruled over by a Leviathan, namely, an autocratic monarch or assembly.

My thesis statement in this essay is that man is the most destructive of all God's creatures which, if true, means that true democracy may be unattainable on this planet. In fact, it could be said that we are in danger of losing not only democracy but the planet itself. My focus here will be on the crisis facing democracy not only in Ireland but globally. History teaches us that man is very good at devising and operating a variety of mechanisms to gain and retain control over people and society. In the past, many of the great leaders were looked upon as gods and as we know, gods can do no wrong.

On would-be gods:

In pagan times, people believed in many gods and divine intervention in the affairs of men. We read about such things in the Greek myths, in the Nordic sagas and in the Celtic lore of Ireland. I expect that many people will have read 'Sapiens' by Yuval N. Harari (2015). There is a great deal of wisdom in the Afterword: 'The Animal that Became a God.' Harari states that in pre-historic times, some 2.5 million years ago, homo sapiens was an ape of no significance in a corner of Africa. 'In the following millennia it transformed itself into master of the entire planet. Today, it stands on the verge of becoming a god …with divine powers of creation and destruction. Unfortunately, the Sapiens regime on earth has produced little that we can be proud of.' (Sapiens, 465).

In essence, Harari is saying two things about modern man. Firstly, and most paradoxically, the very people whose goal is to 'kill' God, want to be gods themselves. And secondly, that man is the most destructive of all God's creatures. Man has little respect for his fellow man or for the planet on which he lives. Students of history can see how proud men and women have always wanted to be revered as gods not only in ancient times but even in modern times. A few examples will suffice to illustrate this point.

The pharaohs in ancient Egypt considered themselves gods. Each pharaoh was said to possess divine status. His wife, the queen, was called 'God's wife'. And of course, the pharaohs were buried in style in giant pyramids in the Valley of the Kings, along with their treasure. One may recall Shelly's famous Ozymandias sonnet about the inevitable decline of great rules with pretentions to greatness such as Ramesses 2, King of Kings.

Claudius Caesar was Roman Emperor from 41 to 54 A. D. While alive, he received the worship of a living 'Princeps' and was revered as 'Claudius the God'. However, his reign was far from godly. Rome under Claudius was a web of corruption, strife, bribery, and cronyism. Seneca mocks the deification of Claudius and states that he was 'an unpleasant fool'.

The Vikings saw themselves as having divine status. They saw themselves as a godly race, Children of Odin, Thor and a dozen lesser Nordic gods. They were a superior race, impervious to the mayhem they were inflicting on the people they terrorised.

During the course of history, we have seen many leaders who claimed to be oracles of a higher power from whom they received licence to terminate unwanted persons. Killing was validated by divine intervention. It was a divine licence to kill the unwanted that motivated such butchers as Attila the Hun, Genghis Khan, the 'sun-king' Louis XIV, Joseph Stalin, Adolf Hitler, and many more terminators. In our own time, we have Kim Jong-un, Supreme Leader of North Korea. His people firmly believe that Kim is a god. He is worshipped as an omnipotent genius. However, we know that he is really a tyrant, well known for purges, human rights violations and executions. He spends billions of won on developing weapons of mass destruction while his people suffer from famine. When you are a god, you can kill unwanted people with impunity. Human killing is the last refuge of the tyrant.

In Japan, Emperor Naruhito is still regarded unabashedly as a living god, even though he has fewer powers than the President of Ireland, who has never claimed to be a Celtic god.

The reader is obviously wondering what all of the above god-talk has to do with the Irish Republic and its rulers in Leinster House. My point is that the 'liberal' leaders of the 'New Ireland' government wants to kill God and the Ten Commandments and impose new norms on society. They want to be gods and they anoint a number of 'little pharaohs' to look after the various Department of government. In fact, those appointed to the Department of Health, the Department of Education and the Department of Social Welfare and Children see themselves as demi-gods. Driven by arrogance and self-delusion, they rule by diktat, doubletalk, distortion and outright lies. The 'little pharaohs', just like the Supreme Leader, know what is best for us, what is in the national interest. When you are a god, you are above reproach and it would be very unwise to question divine authority. The great illusion in Ireland today is thinking that you are in control of your life.

On brute force:

Over the centuries since the earliest times powerful nations have always sought to extend their hegemony over nation of lesser power by way of conquest, colonialism, exploitation, slavery, genocide, mass-killing, ethnic cleansing, torture and detention in concentration camps. Even in prehistoric times, Homo Sapiens soon leaned how to make weapons and build fortifications to defend his territory or to engage in raids on neighbouring territories. Tribal warfare soon became the norm and as smaller states were conquered, great empires sprang up. You can read all about the 'evil empires' in Part 3 of Yuval Harari's history of mankind.[1]

I would ask the reader to pause for a moment and consider the lexicon of violence, crime, mayhem and murder that exists in every language – verbs such as abuse, annihilate, assault, attack, batter, bully, break, coerce, conquer, control, crush, decapitate, destroy, dismember, extort, exterminate, fight, flog, invade, kill, punish, terminate, subjugate, suppress, rape, terminate. The list of adjectives denoting violence is even longer – abusive, aggressive, barbaric, barbarous, bellicose, bloody, bloodthirsty, brutal, cruel, coercive, destructive, evil, ferocious, fierce, furious, gross, homicidal, hostile, inhuman, inhumane, murderous, raging, savage, subhuman, tempestuous, vicious, violent. The Irish language has even a richer vocabulary of violence and oppression by the foreigner ('Gall'), for instance, 'forneart' (force), 'ansmacht' (tyranny), foréigan (violence) and cos ar bolg (victimisation).

All around us we see the destructive legacy of mankind. For centuries, man has been polluting and destroying the planet on which we live, waging war, engaging in inhuman activities – colonialism, slavery, genocide, ethnic cleansing and terrorism. Now, in the modern era, science and technology have made us more deadly, more daring, and more efficient at terminating unwanted persons. Science and technology have become the new god. However, when wisdom, truth and the moral order are set aside, society lapses into barbarism. I am not saying that the Irish government of today uses physical force to suppress the traditional culture, values, human rights and freedom of its citizens. I am, however, saying that it uses something more sinister, namely, propaganda and brainwashing. Its socio-political policy is based on secularism/humanism, an ideology that may be 'liberal' or socialist or evolutionary in origin. It is very good at cooking up the evidence and rationale for its 'health' agenda which legalises the selective killing of unwanted persons at the beginning of life (via abortion) or at the end of life (via euthanasia). Its economic policy is based on neoliberalism which puts money and profit before people. Furthermore, I am saying that it uses every dirty trick in the book to shape public opinion and it uses blatant abuse of power in order to legalise such obscenities as human killing, same-sex marriage, unnatural sexual practices, blasphemy and the perversion of youth. As a result it has, with massive support from the media, created the monster called the 'New Ireland'.

On belief systems:

Homo sapiens has been nurtured, formed and conditioned by a wide range of vastly different belief systems which we now refer to as cultures, religions, or ideologies, all of which are intended to help people interpret reality, to understand the meaning of life and to adopt a set of principles for our moral, social or political wellbeing. They are classified as atheistic, animistic, indigenous, African, political, and religious. Atheists refer to people of faith as 'irrational' because they believe in a Supreme Being (God), spirits, angels, heaven and hell, demons, witches, saints and prophets a 'holy book' of scriptures and the afterlife. They regard all religion as evil - 'the opium of the people' according to Karl Marx. They forget that they also subscribe to a belief system which excludes all religious belief and metaphysical reality. They are wrongly called 'unbelievers'. Depending on their particular political orientation, they are known as secularists, liberals, humanists, socialists, communists, etc. They all share a real hatred of the Abrahamic religions - Christianity, Islam, and Judaism.

Irish culture has been predominately Christian for centuries but over the past fifty years there has been a determined effort by various writers, politicians and disgruntled feminists to denounce religion and people of faith and embrace a new culture of liberalism/secularism. I shall have more to say on the resulting clash of cultures in Essay 4. It is true that religion is a major source of social control. In Ireland some people say that they probably all had too much religion during their formative years. But was it real religion or Victorian morality? There was much outward appearance of piety and sobriety, of dignity and restraint, but little concern for working class welfare, a blindness to child labour, real poverty, greed, and prostitution, all of which are well documented in the writings of Charles Dickens. Hypocrisy and the maintenance of respectability were more evident than real Christian virtue. In Ireland, the Magdalene Laundries and the Mother-and-Baby homes were supported and condoned by the Church and State. Our national ethos had deviated a mile from the 'do unto others' injunction of the Gospel.

On scientism:

The one thing that scientists hate most is philosophy and especially metaphysics, which discusses the questions left unanswered by the particular sciences such as the nature of being and reality, the meaning of life, consciousness, free will, etc. Certain well-known scientists, for instance Richard Dawkins, do not believe in metaphysical reality. They believe only in scientism, that is the assumption that science can answer all the big questions that normal people ask. They believe that all questions can be answered by the scientific method which begins with a question. You then embark on a well-established process of inquiry which entails a precise statement of the nature and scope of the enquiry and the systematic observation, measurement and experiment of the object being observed based on the formulation and testing of your hypothesis. You then begin the laborious task of data collection after which you return to base and analyse your data under strict conditions. Eventually, certain trends in the data will be noticed and recorded and certain conclusions and recommendation can be made. However, Karl Popper refuted the classical scientific method. He pointed out that science is not about certainty. No observation is free from the possibility of error. He demonstrated that one counter-instance falsifies a whole theory. You might, for instance, hypothesise that 'all roses are red'. However, one yellow rose falsifies your hypothesis. Hence, Popper proposed the falsification principle instead of the scientific method.

Science is absolutely necessary in making sense of the physical world and the laws that govern it but it cannot explain such things as consciousness, moral truth, free will, etc. it may tell us how the Big Bang happened, how evolution happened and it may give us very good information about natural phenomena. We all love to watch and listen to Professor Brian Cox on BBC Two as he explains the Wonders of the Universe. However, many hard questions remain unanswered, for instance what happened before the Big Bang? Is there a God? Did God really appear to Moses in the burning bush? What are we to believe about the Bible, or Christian philosophers such as Thomas Aquinas or John Henry Newman who had much to say on the role of conscience and the harmony of faith and reason? Who is telling the truth?

Atheists believe that all knowledge, beliefs and values are social constructs governed by physical laws. They deny the existence of free will. If free will is ruled out, so too is conscience - the moral voice that tells us which things are inherently right or wrong. It is innate morality which enables us to make choices between the opposites, good and evil. Atheists and their liberals/ secularists /humanists seek to exclude moral debate from all areas of public life by supressing the belief system of others while they propagate their own. They often invoke famous words of the German philosopher Friedrich Nietzsche that 'God is dead.' (Gott ist tot.) In 'Thus Spake Zarathustra (1884: section 22) we are told: 'Dead are all the Gods. Now do we desire the Overman to live.' Many people read this as meaning that the new god is science. However, if you read Nietzsche carefully you will see that he was being ironic. He was declaring that 'reason' was dead, that the 'Superman' was a monster and that without a God, the basic belief system of Europe was in jeopardy.

In France, the philosopher and historian Michel Foucault was greatly influenced by Nietzsche's ideas on social control. His most notable work 'Discipline and Punish: The Birth of the Prison' (1975) describes how rulers express their power by violence, punishment, torture and execution.

He used the panopticon[2] as a metaphor in order to illustrate how a government subjugates its citizens and exercises social control through societal institutions.

My final comment on scientism concerns certain ill-informed science-minded writers who refer to people of faith as 'irrational apes' or 'Neanderthals'. Regarding the former, having lived and worked in Borneo for 14 years in close proximity to orang-utans, gibbons and other apes, I happen to know that apes are not at all irrational within their own domain – the rainforest. Moreover, they are family oriented and do not kill their young or their own kind. As David Attenborough has pointed out, we could learn a lot from the great apes. As for the term 'Neanderthal' to denote subhuman species, modern genetic research, published in the journal 'Genetics' indicates that all modern humans, including Irish people, carry some Neanderthal ancestry in their DNA. Hence, writers who claim be to well-informed scientists should not cast aspersions on our remote ancestors; they should look in the mirror.

On brainwashing and propaganda:

You may think that you are in control of your life, but we are all the victims of influencers. Many governments today, including the Irish government, are propped up by the twin pillars of brainwashing and propaganda. Brainwashing is a broad term for the process of pressurising people into adopting radically different beliefs, attitudes or ideology by the use of systematic and often forcible means such as harassment, intimidation, character assassination and detention without trial. We know how the Chinese government brainwashes Uighur Muslims in re-education camps in the Xinjiang region. In November 2019, a BBC Panorama programme revealed how inmates are locked up, indoctrinated and punished in mass detention camps. We know about the Gulag correctional labour camps in former Soviet Union (1930-1955). We know about the shocking harassment and detention of dissident by the Stasi in the former German Democratic Republic. Today, Western government prefer a more subtle form of brainwashing which we call propaganda. They no longer use crude Stasi-esque methods such as an electronic baton to the back of the head. They focus instead on brain-bending, thought reform, re-education and cultural transformation – all of which come under the umbrella of propaganda. Propaganda has two legs; it refers to biased and misleading information which is used to promote a political cause or point of view, and it also refers to the dissemination of such information as a political strategy. In the digital age, dispensing government spin is as easy as taking candy from a kid; one just hits the tweet button on Facebook or Twitter. In the 'New Ireland' there is little real political debate on a rational level. Instead, what we get most of the time is tweeting on social media. Each political party seeks to control the narrative and go after those who think or speak different from their political, social and economic policies. They love to reopen old wounds and present tweets as facts. They never engage with the complexities and legacy issues that have shaped the history of the Republic. They all claim to be the authentic voice of Irish republicanism, carrying the sword of Irish freedom (An Cliamh Solais). What we get is the gutter politics of the TikTok generation – distortion, fake news and linear thinking. People are constantly being assailed by the liberal media, big tech censorship and cancel culture.

George Orwell's novel 'Animal Farm' (1945) is a powerful satire on the cunning and corrupt ruling elite who consolidate power and gradually take away civil rights and liberty while preaching parity of esteem for all. When I hear Irish politicians announcing that 'we are all in this together' I recall Napoleon and Snowball in full flow conditioning their comrades into buying into the new liberal ideology of Manor Farm. The fear factor arising from not supporting the regime easily subverts the voice of the subjects who do not realise that they are being conditioned and manipulated. The 'New Ireland' is a mirror image of the 'Animal Farm'.

That fact explains why in recent times Irish people have given the ruling elite a blank cheque to legislate unspeakable measures which are deemed necessary in a modern 'liberal' state.

The Irish government is very good at brainwashing and propaganda. It does not use lethal force to silence and intimidate dissidents. Instead, it demonises dissidents and their traditional norms and values. It rides roughshod over the traditional values and beliefs of people of faith and it denounces the branch of moral conduct which we call bioethics. It sets out to establish new societal norms. It holds that 'normal people' in the 'New Ireland' have to liberate themselves from the tyranny of the church (and especially the Catholic Church). We are told that the Bible is a fairy-tale, that the Ten Commandments are obsolete and that we have to 'move on' and embrace the secularist gospel of sexual permissiveness, the legalisation abortion, gay marriage, blasphemy, the denial of freedom of conscience, the banning of peaceful protest and secularisation of faith schools. What is truly amazing is that nobody is shouting 'Stop the madness'. The indoctrination is so pervasive that nobody really notices it. We are all its intended audience and its willing subjects. It seems very odd to me that Irish people are willing to be governed by people who celebrate human killing and other gross acts of human perversion.

Irish politicians are very good at the art of persuasion and keeping the rabble in line. They do so with the active support of a compliant media, especially the national broadcaster RTE and most of the national newspapers. The great myth of our time is the assumption that politicians in Ireland and the EU are fulfilling the wishes of the people. In fact, they operate according to a hidden agenda which is autocratic. History shows us how effective propaganda can be. For instance, Joseph Goebbels who was Hitler's Minister of Propaganda, was a superb Nazi activist who exerted control over the news media in Germany. He was greatly admired for his antisemitism and his agenda of cleansing the German nation of unwanted persons, especially Jews and intellectuals. He was a classic terminator of human beings but was he any more vile than current EU states that promote and practise abortion and euthanasia? Liberal Ireland has blood on its hands – the blood of thousands of innocent human lives. The Irish state has 'moved on'. It has legalised human killing.

The fear factor:

The Irish government has come close to achieving autocratic rule. Power resides in the government of the day and the Oireachtas (Parliament) is perilously close to an 'elective dictatorship'. It uses a range of strategies to control people lives. I have already mentioned brainwashing and propaganda and I have referred to several other controlling factors such as obfuscation and lying, fake news and misinformation, self-interest and self-praise, political correctness and fear. Stoking fear is the most obvious tool employed by the ruling elite. Many Irish people seem to be paralysed by fear. They live in fear of not being able to enjoy a normal life due to the housing crisis, the health crisis, the cost of living crisis and the gradual erosion of civil liberties. Young people in particular are traumatised by the lack of affordable housing, unemployment, ill health, destitution and deep anxiety. How long will they remain silent and take dictation from a government lacking moral leadership, honesty and integrity? Fear is not an inevitable part of the human condition. It has to be subordinated to a higher power. Human beings need divine intervention in order rise above poverty, injustice, hardship and oppression. People of faith do not fear. They say: 'The Lord is my shepherd, I shall not fear.' Therefore, they choose faith, not fear. I am convinced that the grace of God dispels fear. A strong Christian faith is a channel to personal peace and wellbeing. I cannot say that Ireland is a failed state. However, it seems that many Irish people have lost the faith and accept the secularist ideology of arrogant politicians with no concern for truth and common decency.

The pernicious media

The real power brokers in the world today are the media. They have enormous influence over people's lives and that is why the government's press office courts them. Governments today are guided by public opinion and not by principle. They prefer prejudice to principle and they put their political survival above the common good. The national newspapers and the national broadcaster (RTE) seem eager to advocate the disintegration of Christian Ireland and actively endorse the rise of secular humanism. They ignore the fact that about 80% of Irish people are Catholic, at least in name, and another 10% belong to other religions. Catholics today may not be regular church goes, but they still wish to retain their Catholic traditions and have their children educated in a Christian ethos.

The silent church

What is most surprising is that church leaders have remained almost silent on moral issues. I know of only one bishop who has spoken out against abortion. He is Bishop Kevin Doran. In January 2018, he correctly predicted that the rationale that was used to justify abortion would be used to justify ending the lives of frail older people and individuals with significant disability. He pointed out that it was a grave error for the silent majority to give politicians in Leinster House a blank cheque to introduce whatever abortion scheme they chose at any time in the future. And of course he was absolutely right; 'liberal' politicians legalised wide-ranging abortion, infanticide and are about to legalise euthanasia / assisted suicide. People of faith should be outraged but their silence on these issues has been deafening. Some Irish pastors are saying that we should not protests too loudly about abortion because 'women know best'; they are no longer saying that life is God's gift and that all life is sacred. But corruption in the church is not something new; it has a long history.

In subsequent essays I shall have more to say on three other major forms of brainwashing. They are (a) the outsourcing of controversial issues in society to a spurious unelected body called a 'Citizens' Assembly', which was invented by the government as a means of shaping public opinion. In the case of abortion, obviously, no Irish government would want to be remembered as the government that legalised human killing. Hence, it was a good cop-out to create an outside body which would create a rationale for abortion. We were told that the work of the Citizens' Assembly would be 'an exercise in deliberative democracy'. It was of course, exactly the opposite. (b) If the Citizen's Assembly was farcical, the Joint Oireachtas which followed and ratified its findings was even more so. I shall show how that parliamentary body was rigged; in fact, it was reduced to a kangaroo court which paved the way for the government to legalise human killing. (c) Education or rather re-education has always been a fertile ground for indoctrination by governments. The one thing liberals and secularists hate is moral formation and hence they will not rest until Religious Instruction is marginalised or possibly removed from the curriculum.

Modern so-called 'liberal progressives' regard religion, moral formation, tradition and culture as obstacles to progress. They do not seems to realize that we are shaped and moulded by our cultural heritage. Our belief system, our native language, our myths and legend have a profound impact on our national psyche. Our ancient religious values are based on the Judeo-Christian scriptures and they keep us grounded in modern times, when false prophets and fake ideologies seek to lead us astray. Edmund Burke repeatedly stressed to importance of maintaining our traditional moral values, and the Austrian composed Gustav Mahler famously said: 'Tradition is not the worship of ashes, but the preservation of fire.'

Most of us think that we are in control of our lives. However, we are in fact influenced and controlled by government propaganda, by fake news and by social media tweets. As a result, many Irish people today are subject to massive self-delusion. Nobody is asking the key question: Who is shaping the 'New Ireland'? It is obvious to me that a hidden hand is secretly moulding the epistemological and ethical beliefs of Irish people.

Endnotes:

1   Yuval N. Harari (2015). 'Sapiens: A Brief History of Humankind'. London: Vantage
2   Panopticon: A circular prison with cells arranged around a central observation tower from which prisoners could at all times be observed but could not see into the tower

4

THE CLASH OF CULTURES

'Culture is the root of politics, and religion is the root of culture.'

Richard John Neuhaus.

The purpose of this essay is to describe the clash of cultures that is currently raging in Ireland and to briefly review the emerging evidence for the so-called 'New World Order'. The problem is Europe today is that there is profound clash between two diametrically opposed political forces, namely liberal/secularist culture (aka Liberal Democracy) and traditional Christian culture (aka Christian Democracy). It is an over-simplification, of course, since on purely economic criteria it is the old clash between right-wing conservatism (i.e. wealth) and left-wing socialism (poverty). Both of these cultures have a populist fringe which on the right is marked by extreme nationalism and on the left by neo-Marxism. The salient feature of Liberal Democracy is secularism. What is strange about all of this is the fact that secularism is shared by both right-wing capitalists and left-wing socialists – very odd bedfellows. What unites them is profound anti-religious prejudice which is mainly overt Christo-phobia i.e. hatred of all things Christian but it also includes Islamophobia and anti-Semitism. Modern 'liberals' wish to create a secularist state and stamp out every existing religious ethos in public life. The word 'liberal' has lost its original meaning and has become a pejorative term for intolerant secularist ideology. It is unclear which of these opposing forces will win the day. People of faith do not want to be governed by 'liberal' secularists or socialist bigots. Secular people do not want to be governed by people of faith or religious extremists. There does not seem to be a middle way.

Liberal democracy:

Liberal Democracy is the system of government currently in fashion in most western countries including Ireland. It should not be confused with Representative Democracy - a system of government based on democratic consent, i.e. the will of the people. In recent years, Representative Democracy has taken a severe bashing from the two opposing sides of the political spectrum, the extreme right (+ neo-liberalism) and the extreme left (+ neo-Marxism). These two strands, however, have something in common; both ideologies are doctrinaire and secularist, united in their hatred of traditional values, especially Christian values. Their ultimate objective is the cultural transformation of every Christian nation into a secularist state. Modern liberalism is a new cult based on secularist ideology. It is utterly illiberal - the very opposite of classical liberalism. Is seeks to establish a new world order by tearing down all the established institutions, cutting all links with the past, rewriting the Constitution and inventing a whole new language of political discourse, the key words of which are 'secular, inclusive, modern, and progressive' – roughly the same notions of 'liberté, égalité and fraternité' that inspired the French Revolution.

Neoliberalism:

The economics of right-wing 'liberals' is known as neoliberalism. As stated in my glossary, neoliberalism is a form of modern liberalism tending to favour free market capitalism. It is defined by George Monbiot as follows[1]: 'Neoliberalism is the ideology developed by people such as Friedrich Hayek and Milton Friedman. It is not just a set of free-market ideas, but a focused discipline, deliberately applied around the world. It treats competition as humanity's defining characteristic and 'the market' as society's organising principle. The market, it claims, sorts us into a natural hierarchy of winners and losers. Any attempt by politics to intervene disrupts the discovery of this natural order.' Good examples of neoliberalism are Brexit in the UK and Trumpism in the USA. In several EU countries, neoliberalism has become ossified and is considered an absolutist, failed system. However, it seems to be very much alive in Ireland on the right of the political spectrum.

Neo-Marxism:

Neo-Marxism refers to the overthrow of capitalism by the proletariat. It exists to a greater or lesser extent in all of our left-of-centre political parties - Labour, People Before Profit and Social Democrats. Left wing rhetoric is loud, assertive, and delights in taking a chainsaw to its opponents. It seems to have a great appeal for fake feminists, media people, academics, celebrities and university students. Neoliberalism and neo-Marxism are on the same page when it comes to social policy resulting in a system of government that is totally secularist in orientation. That system is known as Liberal Secularism.

Liberal Secularism:

The salient features of modern Liberal Secularism are the following:
It is top down and not bottom up. Political power is held by the few over the many. The inner circle at the top table decides what is best for society. Their logic is impervious to reason. It goes something like this: 'Our laws are right because we say they are right and we know best'.

The doctrine of the sovereignty of parliament is absolute. It is disrespectful of the views and voice of the people. Members of parliament are whipped into conformity. Its leadership operates by stealth, disinformation, fake news, spin, downright lies and euphemism. They pretend to stand for democracy. However, pretence is familiar trait of Irish politics. Politicians belonging to different political creeds cling to each other out of self-interest. Politically, they are miles apart but the common denominator binding them is Liberal Secularism.

Neoliberalism leaves economic development to market forces, which means that wealth is controlled by big business groups (banks, corporations, insurance companies, property developers etc.) which have no interest in redistributing wealth, resulting in the economics of inequality.

The government preaches equality and tolerance but its equality and tolerance are one-sided. Dissidents are not tolerated. Its inner circle abhors religion and people of faith. It seeks to suppress moral formation in faith schools by a brainwashing programme known as RSE.

It is anti-Christian in general and anti-Catholic in particular. The right wing is populist and ultra nationalist and the left wing is secularist and anti-Semitic. To show its utter contempt for people of faith, it has legalised wide-ranging abortion, same-sex marriage, blasphemy and it is planning to legalise 'assisted suicide'. It has little regard for human life. Since human killing is now legal, the government has the power to decide who lives or dies in the 'New Ireland'.

It creates popular consent to its secularist legislation by devious means. It outsources controversial socio-political issues to a farcical non-elected body called the 'Citizens' Assembly' which is an echo chamber for its covert 'liberal' policies.

Counter-culture:

Sociology has a lot to say about counter-culture in general and specifically about the rise of counter-culture in Britain and Ireland during the 60s. It was essentially an anti-Establishment cultural phenomenon, a protest movement against the mainstream social and political norms as ordained by the government (in Ireland, the Oireachtas) and enforced by the courts, the church, local authorities and government agencies. It was anti-capitalism, anti-religion, anti-racism, anti-war, anti-censorship and anti-conservatism and tradition. It wanted fundamental social and political change and it demanded civil rights, equality, freedom of speech, socialism, sexual liberation and the decriminalisation of psychedelic drug use. However, the original hippie counter-culture become a spent force by the mid-70s. After joining the EEC in 1973, Irish people became more European in outlook. more liberal on social issues, more secularist, more humanist and more culturally 'woke'. Counter-culture seemed to have disappeared but in fact it survived in a new and different form, a 'woke' form of liberalism which demanded the legalisation of abortion, same-sex marriage, euthanasia, social pluralism and a host of new social norms under the heading of 'political correctness.' Modern counter-culture is no longer punk subculture. What is extraordinary is that the greatest promoter of counter-culture in the 'New Ireland' is the government. It is the culture of the Establishment. Counter-culture has become, ironically, the dominant culture of the 'New Ireland.' What were once separate subcultures or bubbles have amalgamated into a single homogenous culture, which is transmitted by all of the following:

1. The government (the Oireachtas): Irish parliamentary democracy has never been representative. It has always been top down, not bottom up. The system is rigged in favour of the elite, the wealthy, the fixers, and 'gombeen' men and women. The government, however, sets the headline for the state and it demands unqualified

support for its programme for government which is 'liberal' and secularist so as to retain power by populist support.

2. The media are fully supportive of the liberal/ secularist transformation of the Irish Republic. The feature writers of the mainstream newspapers vie with each other in their promotion of secularist drivel. The old concept of balanced journalism does not apply in the 'New Ireland'. What one gets is mostly fake news from the national broadcaster RTE, the print media, so-called celebrities and academics.

3. Social media platforms - Instagram, YouTube, Facebook, Twitter and TikTok - are a major source of cultural transmission. They are not neutral. They are just as biased as the print media. Facebook and Twitter censor pro-life content but do not censor liberal fake news. All of them are widely used by sexual predators to prey on children and teenagers. Children are growing up in a world of social media and sex websites that steal and exploit photos and details of under-age Irish boys and girls.

4. Ireland if famous for its literary giants - its great novelists, poets, dramatists and short story writers. However, it seems that many publishers have caught the 'liberal' bug and it is now mandatory for would-be authors to submit work which approves of the ethos and aspirations of secularist culture. Good writing is now evaluated on political criteria. While insisting on free speech as a fundamental of secularist ideology, publishers at present act like political puritans and will not accept creative writing that is deemed contrary to the woke movement of the 'New Ireland'.

The problem is that neither the 'New Ireland' nor the EU understand the importance and depth of national culture. Christianity has been around for two thousand years and Europe was a Christian continent until recent times. The EU bosses in Brussels ignore the cultural dimension. The master plan is to create a new unified Europe based on economic principles, but it ignores the cultural foundation. It is utterly absurd to assume that each member state should renounce its centuries-old Judeo-Christian culture and be integrated into a one-size-fits-all superstate. It is hardly surprising that we are now seeing the great EU project breaking up. The founding fathers of the EU tried to create a secularist /socialist Europe. They failed to understand that political stability depends on respect for culture, for tradition, for religion, for laws, for all the cultural elements that make up national sovereignty. In EU ideology the nation-state must be diminished. People must not be allowed to bring Christian thinking into the public square. The approved political dogma is secularism. Progressive EU member states must walk away from their ancient Judeo-Christian ethics, culture and tradition. However, it is obvious that the great majority of Irish people are deeply religious. They have never debated or assented to the exclusion of religion from public life.

Language transmits values, laws, cultural norms and taboos. The Irish language speaks with reference of God, of religion, of holy things, customs and rituals. Irish identity and culture are deeply embedded in the supernatural going back to Celtic times. It will take more than tweets from government ministers to change the native culture of Irish people. Of course, by devious means the governments can change the laws and the Constitution. They may even succeed in persuading themselves and the electorate that certain traditional beliefs and values are outdated and must be replaced by new 'liberal' norms. We know now how socio-cultural indoctrination enabled the Irish government to pass the controversial abortion law.

The abortion issue:

More than any other socio-political issue, the government's promotion of abortion shows its utter disregard for traditional Irish culture. It stands out as the greatest exemplar of barbarism that we have seen since the

Great Famine in Ireland, or the Holocaust in Europe or the more recent genocides in Africa and Asia.

In an essay in 1946, George Orwell stated: 'In our time, political speech and writing are largely the defence of the indefensible.' That statement is especially apt in relation to the Irish government's zealous promotion of abortion. Abortion is about the deliberate killing of the unborn. However, that central fact is not mentioned by the government at all. Instead, our pro-abortion TDs and Senators resort to euphemisms and use deliberately opaque phrases to describe abortion as 'healthcare' or 'human rights' or 'reproductive rights'. They never refer to 'the unborn child', but to the 'foetus' as if it was a half-formed thing which becomes human only at birth. They do not speak of 'killing the unborn' but prefer the phrase 'terminating pregnancy' as if pregnancy was an abstract notion. When abortion is re-defined and dressed up as a merciful medical intervention necessary for the health and wellbeing of women in a crisis pregnancy, the focus on killing is not just de-emphasised, it is removed altogether. Moreover, abortionists glibly use the phrase 'fatal foetal abnormality' for a life-limiting malformation of the foetus even though no such condition exists in medical science. They call themselves 'pro-choice' but no person has the 'choice' to terminate another human being. Since the mass-murder of innocent human life is one of the salient characteristics of Liberal Secularism, I shall discuss it further in a later essay.

Classical liberalism:

Secularists see themselves as 'liberal'- a word which now signifies the opposite of real liberalism, which is known as classical liberalism, 'bleeding-heart liberalism', or 'natural liberty'. John Locke, who founded liberalism, held that each man has a natural right to life, liberty and property. He held that governments must not violate those basic human rights but that is precisely what modern liberalism does. The same idea is found in Adam Smith and John Stuart Mill.[2] Central to classical liberalism is the principle that government must not do harm to people but rather represent their wishes. Moreover, one man's liberty must never impinge on another man's liberty. The current social, economic, political and cultural chaos in the world is the perversion of the term 'liberal' to mean the opposite of its original meaning. The thing called 'modern liberalism' has created worldwide inequality, repression and spiritual emptiness. It is built on false assumptions about the nature of individual freedom. It is full of contradictions. It champions individual choice but dictates and enforces secularist policy. It calls for equal rights but fosters inequality. It adopts 'progressive' social policies but it disintegrates society. If you do not believe me, you should read what learned professors have to say on the subject, for instance, Professor Deneen[3] in his classic book 'Why Liberalism Failed'. Freedom of speech, freedom of religion and the most fundamental freedom of all, the right to life, are denied in the modern version of liberalism, which we call secularism. Another scholar who has written about modern liberalism is Charles Taylor[4], who suggests that religion cannot be excised from human consciousness and from all areas of social and political life. He states that humans have an innate orientation towards 'transcendence' which he defines as 'some yearning for meaning that goes above and beyond the merely human.' If governments were to reset the role of government along the liberal lines suggested by John Locke, Adam Smith and John Stuart Mill, the world would not be in such a mess. The concept of the common good has been lost and laws are no longer based on moral values. The secularist State does not ask: what is a human being? What are the basic rights of a human being by virtue of being human? How can basic human rights be protected under the law? For centuries, the answer was to enshrine fundamental rights in the Constitution. However, the government of the Irish Republic has turned the clock back. It alone will determine which rights are retained or removed from the Constitution. From now on, laws will be based on subjective choice - the desires, interests and ideology of a particular group - the 'liberal' elite. When the concept of the common good is lost, we end up with wrong and harmful decisions. We can no longer say that something is 'right' or 'wrong', 'true' or 'false' because it is all relative. We can no longer trust in the justice and goodness of the laws enacted by the Oireachtas. Moral uncertainty creates a crisis of trust in the entire legal system of a secularised society based on individual choice. When law is not based on values, it has no validity or permanence. A proposal can be voted into law one year and voted out the next.

The New World Order:

At one time it was assumed that the New World Order (NWO) was a right-wing conspiracy invented by social science writers like H. G. Wells in 'The Time Machine' (1895), Aldous Huxley in 'Brave New World' (1932) and George Orwell in 'Nineteen Eighty-four' (1949). However, now we know that it is real. It is the unseen and very secretive body in charge of the cultural, political and economic revolution which is happening worldwide. It operates through several front organisations such as the UN, the WHO, the G-20 leaders, the IMF, and the EU. It is driven by atheists, secularists, liberals, progressives, big corporations, feminists, greedy bankers, corrupt politicians, Freemasonry and the LGBT movement. In essence, it is an untouchable and invisible oligarchy. Its goal is the eradication of the nation-state and its replacement by a global secularist government whose ideology is globalisation and neoliberalism. It is known as a 'shadow government' dedicated to the establishment of Utopian world government based secularist and 'liberal' ideology. Modern liberalism is deeply illiberal. It uses overt brainwashing and indoctrination to propagate its mission and it uses 'political correctness' to silence and demonise its critics. It will not tolerate free speech or freedom of conscience. Any person who upholds traditional moral values is denounced as a bigot, racist, homophobe, xenophobe, etc. It operates under the radar and, like the deadly COVID virus, it infects every corner of society. Its salient characteristics are following:

1. Fake news, lies, misinformation and euphemism. We are now living is a post-truth society. Those who speak the truth are demonised. For instance, it calls abortion 'reproductive health' and it speaks of 'abortion care' as if killing unborn babies was the state's caring duty. It hates free speech and it imposes a no-platforming rule on public media and universities for all genuine democratic voices.

2. Its ideology is secularist. It tells people how to liberate themselves from the tyranny of religion. People of faith are called 'irrational'. It sees no contradiction between telling people to make their own ethical choices while at the same time dictating what those choices should be. It prescribes how people must think, speak and behave by following the wise path mapped out by the illuminati.

3. It believes in massive state indoctrination and brainwashing. It not only uses the media to propagate its ideology, it owns the media. It aims to secularise education and all government-funded bodies and services.

4. One of its main targets is population control which it implements by the selective termination of excess human beings by means of abortion, family planning programmes and euthanasia.

5. It is all for globalisation and the economics of inequality. It controls and dominates world trade and practices economic strangulation of states that do not subscribe to New World dogma.

6. Like the deadly COVID-19 virus, it is in the air we breathe. In the Republic, it permeates all branches of government, local councils, the judiciary, the media, even the churches. Some people have begun to react to its patronage of woke insanity, the 'cancel

culture' stance of journalists and celebrities who often appear on RTE telling us how wonderful the 'liberal' New Ireland is.

The new age of enlightenment:

Clearly, everything about the New World Order and its Irish counterpart, the so-called 'New Ireland' is the very antithesis of representative democracy, the sovereignty of the nation-state and the ethical principles of a true republic. The Irish Republic was founded on Christian principles which hold that man is both body and soul. The soul - the spiritual part - is immortal. Irish people used to believe that humans were created by God and 'unto God they shall return' when their earthly span is run. The secularist view is that God does not exist. and that creation is a myth. The human person is not a spiritual being. Secularists believe that Darwin was right. Human life evolved over millennia from lower forms of life. Home sapiens is an accident of evolution. The human person is no more than a 'vessel of clay'.

The basic principle of liberal secularism is totalitarian equality which can be achieved only by cleansing society of all religious influence. The State must, therefore, undo all the sacred cows of Christian tradition. It must somehow bring about a French Revolution, without the bloodshed and mayhem, of course. A liberal government must transform the national psyche by promoting a tolerance of things that were previously deemed immoral, such as same-sex marriage, access to abortion, blasphemy etc. In the cult of secularism, you make your own morality. You are no longer bound by the Biblical injunctions called The Ten Commandments. According to humanists and secularists, the Ten Commandments were given to Moses a long time ago and no longer apply in our modern secular world. Sociologists tell us that that society has 'moved on' – a phrase much used by Irish politicians. According to the humanist thinking, God does not exist and that the Bible story is pure mythology. We are told that the

Abrahamic scriptures are interesting but must not be regarded in any sense as having truth value. They were composed by demented Orientals wandering about in the hot desert between the Red Sea and the Jordan valley. According to the secularist script, if we abolish faith schools and ban the holy books of Christians, Jews and Muslims, we are on the road to secularist uniformity and society is liberated from the superstitious beliefs and practices of the past. In secularist ideology, there is no metaphysical reality. Humans live on this planet as best they can, guided by science and reason. Then they die and return to elemental dust. There is no winding stairs to a heavenly home beyond the blue horizon and belief in a place or state called 'hell' is nothing more than biblical mythology.

Of course, galloping secularism is not a new development. According to Baruch Spinosa, one of the great rationalists of the 17th century, God is certainly not a creator but the sum of the natural and physical laws of the universe. He goes on to say that good and evil are nothing more than modes of thinking and that you should live according to your nature. We can infer that humanists, like Spinosa, do not believe in the afterlife. Humans should enjoy the now, forget about happiness, wisdom and fulfilment. They are just animals. I am not sure that Spinosa would have been perfectly at home in the 'New Ireland'. One must ask whether it is in the nature of man to kill his fellow man? I think Spinosa would draw the line at human killing. I think he would say that taking human life is not something that humans are programmed to do. After all, Homo Sapiens is supposed to act rationally and live in peace with his fellow man. It is in the nature of man to act rationally but terminating a human life can hardly be said to come within the scope of rationality.

A Christian perspective:

I do not pay much attention to the ethical philosophy coming from the mouth of the apostles of secularism / humanism. They are profoundly ignorant of theology and I suspect that they have never read the Bible nor any other holy book. It is impossible to argue with people who do know what they are arguing against. What is especially appalling in Ireland is the self-delusion and hypocrisy of the ruling class. They are 'whited sepulchres' (Matthew 23:27), outwardly virtuous but inwardly corrupt. Nobody likes hypocrites. What they want is a 'progressive', 'liberal' church which condones abortion, euthanasia, eugenics, blasphemy and sexual practices against the order of nature. Anyone who questions the word of God in the Bible cannot be called a person of faith, much less a Christian. Secularism has little appeal for people of faith. The Irish psyche is comfortable with faith in God and a moral code based on the sacred scriptures, which contain wisdom, enlightenment, tolerance and respect for all living creatures. The Irish live by faith. Their culture and native language show enormous respect for sacred scripture and the presence of God not only in church but everywhere. The Irish language is not only a classical language but also a repository of Christian culture. For centuries Irish Catholics defended their faith in spite of 'dungeon, fire and sword.' They honoured Daniel O'Connell, the Liberator, who in 1929 won Catholic Emancipation and the repeal of the remaining Penal Laws.[5] At present, their faith is once more under attack not by a foreign power but by the enemy within - the secularist ruling elite in Leinster House. In the 'New Ireland' we are looking at moral depravity on a grand scale. We are seeing the erosion of compassion, civility, honour, respect, kindness, wisdom and truth. A society that has lost respect for the sacredness of life is doomed. What we find in our modern 'liberal' State is dehumanisation spreading like a tidal wave from the seat of government to every corner of society.

The one thing you can safely say about the current 'liberal' government of the Republic is that it is utterly illiberal. It will not tolerate dissent from its secularist ideology and it will do its utmost to silence those whose ideology is different from its version. Its primary focus is on propagating its ideology and not looking after the welfare and betterment of the people that is elected to serve. Its agenda is the deconstruction of Christian Ireland. As a result of persistent indoctrination and lying by the government and the secular media, Irish people have lost personal sovereignty, integrity and national sovereignty. They now live in a ghost republic - a fake-liberal republic known as the 'New Ireland'. However, we have seen how many dictatorial governments tumble when ordinary people realise that they are not powerless. We should not forget how Václav Havel's Greengrocer [6] manged to withstand the oppressive Czech dictatorship. We could learn a lot from Havel's Greengrocer. We are not powerless. We must not succumb to political apathy. We should remember the wise words of Edmund Burke: 'The only thing necessary for the triumph of evil is for good men to do nothing.'

End notes:

1   George Monbiot: 'The Guardian Journal' 11.9.2019, p. 4

2   William Letwin (1988). 'Traditions of Liberalism: Essays on John Locke, Adam Smith and John Stuart Mill'. New South Wales: Centre for Independent Studies

3   Patrick J. Deneen (2018). 'Why Liberalism Failed'. Yale University Press.

4   Abbey, R. (2007). 'Charles Taylor: Canadian philosopher'. Online Encyclopaedia Britannica. Retrieved. 15.11.2020

5   Penal Laws: A series of laws imposed on Irish Catholics over the period 1695-1829 in an attempt by the Crown to stamp out 'popery'.

6   Václav Havel's Greengrocer: In an essay entitled 'The Power of the Powerless' (1978) Havel uses the parable of the greengrocer to illustrate how ordinary people can 'live in truth' under an oppressive regime. The greengrocer places in his shop window the slogan: 'Workers of the world, unite!' which seems to signal conformity to the system but the real meaning is not conveyed by the printed words. The greengrocer conceals his fear of being branded a 'dissident' by a slogan which local people and the Czech Security Forces read differently.

For more on the clash of cultures in Ireland see John Waters 'Ireland, an Obituary', 28 May 2018. Available online on the First Things website.

5

THE NEW IRELAND

In this essay the focus is on the 'New Ireland' that has been emerging over the past twenty-five years. I have to admit that many things have changed for the better in the Republic. The economy was in good shape up to the onset of the Coronavirus epidemic, which is predicted to cause a global recession in 2021 and possibly longer. The Republic is now a prosperous country. There is very little unemployment as in former times. Irish towns and cities now have top class hotels, mega shopping centres, state-of-the-art sporting venues, excellent schools and colleges and vibrant cultural events. However, some things have not changed at all. The rich still get richer and the poor get poorer. Many young families are finding it hard to make ends meet. The cost of housing has reached astronomical levels and even two salaries are insufficient to pay the mortgage, the property tax, school fees, child care and the ever-increasing utility bills. Many families are living in fear of eviction and the prospect of having to live in shoe-box emergency accommodation or worse still join the homeless sleeping in the street or in shelters provided by charities. Ireland is a wealthy nation but almost half the population is living in near poverty. The Irish economy is a basket case of boom and bust, bailout and austerity – 'the economics of inequality'[1] which may be summarised as follows:

- Crony capitalism vs poverty and austerity

- Insiders vs outsiders; those in the money vs those on the margin
- Variances in income and ownership of capital
- Neoliberalism vs strong anti-establishment sentiment. People want a stake; they want to end the great wealth divide. They demand efficient redistribution of the nation's wealth.
- Unjust and unfair taxes especially the property tax, USC and VAT on goods and services
- The lack of affordable housing and rent control
- The lack of an efficient national health service and especially poor provision for mental health
- The slow death of rural Ireland; the closing of rural schools, post offices and Garda stations
- Poor infrastructure especially broadband, flood protection and an efficient and affordable national bus and train service

Irish workers give the government almost half of their income but in return they get very little unlike workers in other EU countries. Sadly, the incompetence of Irish politicians is proverbial. Each political party looks after its own tribe and the vested interest of its members is paramount. The result is a national paralysis, with the political elite in power spending lavishly on vanity projects while ordinary people are bled dry.

Rural Ireland is being systematically wiped out. Many rural towns are stagnating, starved of investment. The government has shut down many local post offices, the local Garda stations, the local dispensary and the local school. The family farm has been an integral part of rural Ireland for centuries but small farms are being phased out by a new breed of Irish landlords whose mass production methods of farming show scant regard for the environment or for the welfare of the community. Goldsmith's poem about the 'The Deserted Village', is as true today as it was 200 years ago. It speaks of rural depopulation, the pursuit of excessive wealth by greedy landlords and the indifference of an uncaring government. Obviously, in the digital age one cannot return to the pastoral Ireland of

1770 but the government has no brief to systematically destroy a way of life based on honest labour, the goodness of rural people, their moral and cultural values and the genuine goodness of their lives. Many people in low- lying areas live in fear of flooding every winter as they wait in vain for flood protection.

The Irish government today shows scant regard for social equality and social justice. Many of our TDs and Senators seem to have lost all moral compass. They have become arrogant, uncaring, mean-spirited and godless. The national mood has also changed for the worse. I no longer see smiling Irish eyes in the street. I see rude people, staring into their mobile phones, never saying a civil word to each other. Their body language and attire speak volumes about their profound disenchantment. What I find most distressing is Ireland descent into secularism. By that, I mean living without God. I have been reading a very interesting book about the 'New Ireland' by David Quinn. His book is called 'How we killed God'.[2] Its thesis is that our government and its backers have set out to kill the idea of God by marginalising religion from public life. A new sterile groupthink has replaced our Christian values and heritage. A secularist elite is now at the helm of 'the ship of fools' resulting in unchallenged, poor-quality decision-making. For me, the most bizarre aspect of Ireland's descent into secularism is its total disregard for human life. I find it beyond belief that Irish people should welcome with open arms a culture of death. Clearly, something quite radical has happened in the Irish psyche which has given the government a blank cheque to legalise human killing. I watched in horror the obscene victory celebrations outside Dublin Castle as the result of referendum on the abortion issue was announced. I saw government ministers hugging each other and dancing in the great square. Of course, I am all for celebrating when we have something of value to celebrate, like winning the World Cup but only morons would celebrate the legalisation of human killing.

The 20th December 2018 was a sad day for Ireland. On that day, the President signed into law the abortion Bill giving the parliament the right to 'terminate' unwanted unborn babies. We all know the meaning of the verb 'terminate' and we all know what terminators do. The history of mankind in rich in terminators. Now, as a result of the Health Abortion Act, 2018, human killing is legal in the Republic of Ireland. The secular media and feminists see the legalisation of abortion as the great step forward - the crowning achievement of the 'New Ireland'. Killing an unwanted unborn human being is now a woman's choice. The Abortion Act shows the world how the 'New Ireland' has moved. For pro-life people, however, it remains the vilest Act of parliament ever enacted since the legalisation of slavery.

The legalisation of abortion was sold to the public as a Health Act. Now, the shocking reality of abortion has become evident for all to see. It is about the mass killing of unwanted, unborn babies. And still nobody is talking about the intentional killing of 6,666 Irish pre-born babies in 2019. Of course, it was not the will of the people. It was the will of the Oireachtas and the godfathers of abortion, as well as a highly organised pro-abortion campaign.

In the 'New Ireland' we no longer have representative democracy. Only people in the inner circle know what is going on. Members of parliament propose but the inner circle disposes. All policy is top down, not bottom up as in a real democracy. Consequently, the form of government that shapes the 'New Ireland' may be described as follows:

1. Its main feature is a pronounced 'democratic deficit' by which I mean lack of democratic accountability and control of the decision-making process. That explains why our State institutions fail to function properly. Policy is decided at the top table.

2. The doctrine of the sovereignty of parliament is axiomatic. It is the parliament that is sovereign, not 'the people'. (cf. A. C. Grayling, 2017: 132-3) Political parties have their 'whips' to ensure

attendance at crucial votes on key issues. Dissenters are silenced or expelled from the party.

3. Nepotism and cronyism undermine any pretence of representative democracy. Cronies are appointed to positions of authority regardless of their qualifications. No matter how incompetent a government Minister is, he or she is rarely fired.

4. The political elite in power is blind to the real concerns of ordinary people. I am referring to the thousands of people who are homeless or living in emergency accommodation. I am referring to the national health service which is on brink of collapse. I am referring to the growing levels of crime in every town and city. In the 'New Ireland' somebody gets killed almost every day. Rural Ireland is dying on its feet but the government keeps closing down local schools, post offices and Garda stations. Its main focus is propagating its secularist agenda - its cultural revolution. But for hundreds of charities, many families would face destitution.

5. The government functions in devious ways. It is very good at brainwashing, spinning and transforming peoples' attitudes on specific issues, such as abortion, faith schools, blasphemy, etc. It works in collusion with the media to make fake news, lies and soundbites sound credible. Moreover, the poverty of real debate in parliament is stunning. Members read aloud from a prepared text and hardly ever deviate into sense.

6. The government likes to outsource complex issues to a new body called a Citizens' Assembly which was designed to present government policy in a favourable light. It is a total cop-out by which 99 citizens, instead of parliament, are persuaded to vote in favour of a particular government policy and their recommendations are taken as divine revelation. Of course, that body has neither the competence nor the authority to formulate government policy.

7. The toxic tentacles of the central government reach to every corner of the country and to every County Council. On social issues, the government sees which way the wind is blowing and jumps on the populist bandwagon acceding to the demands of lobbyists who spend vast amounts of time and money selling their particular agenda.

8. The government does not like to be answerable to the Constitution. It will, therefore, regularly amend it and eventually tear it up. The idea of enshrining fundamental human rights is a Constitution is anathema to a government which seeks to retain power by legalising 'liberal' issues, such as blasphemy, abortion, same-sex marriage, assisted dying, and 'objective' sex education in schools.

9. The 'New Ireland' is not an abode of peace. It is torn between two extreme political ideologies - right-wing neoliberalism and left-wing neo-Marxism. The traditional Christian centre is being squeezed into oblivion by secularists at both ends of the political spectrum.

10. The only important values in life are truth, integrity and wisdom. However, those attributes no longer exist in the 'New Ireland'. Everything about the 'New Ireland' is fake. The former Taoiseach rightly describes modern Irish liberalism as 'a quiet revolution' very different from the cultural revolution that Mao Zedong implemented in China. However, there is a difference. Whereas Chairman Mao sought to change the public sphere of the nation, the 'New Ireland' cultural revolution seek to change the private sphere of the individual.

11. Central to secularist ideology is the idea that religion must not be taught or practised. God and the Bible must be banished from society. One way to 'kill God' is by secularising the school curriculum. A secularist Department of Education will do its utmost to marginalise the teaching of religion and scripture in schools. In the 'New Ireland' a new subject called RSE has been

added to the curriculum in all Primary and Secondary schools. Its goal is blatant indoctrination of the most perverse kind, which I shall return to in a later essay. Another target of curricular reform concerns the teaching of history. Socialist/secularist governments are good at erasing history. A former Irish Education Minister removed the teaching of history from the Secondary school curriculum. Many people were mystified as to the motivation for such a move. Could it be that the history of Ireland is reflective of the values and culture of a Christian nation, something that is anathema to a devout socialist? In the 'New Ireland' is it necessary to erase all traditional notions of identity, belonging and patriotism. Irish patriotism, Irish culture and the Irish language are deeply embedded in traditional Catholicism and enlightened Protestantism.

12. In the 'New Ireland' many TDs and Senators pontificate about the pernicious influence of the Catholic Church and the need to marginalise the teaching of religion in schools under Catholic patronage. However, the same TDs and Senators sit on their fat backsides while charities such as the Vincent de Paul, Crosscare, Focus Ireland, the Peter McVerry Trust, Merchants Quay Ireland, Brother Kevin's Capuchin Day Centre and Trócaire are out there on the front line providing accommodation, free meals, food banks and medical aid to the poorest and most destitute members of society. Consequently, it can be concluded that the so-called 'New Ireland' is no longer a true republic; it is a dysfunctional secularist State.

Endnotes:

1   Thomas Piketty (2015). 'The Economics of Inequality'. Cambridge, Mas.: The Belknap Press of Harvard University Press.

2   David Quinn (2017). 'How we killed God'. Dublin: Currach Press.

6

RELIGION, FAITH AND FAMILY

The relationship between Church and State in Ireland has always been fraught. The spiritual concerns of the church and the temporal concerns of the State frequently clash and sometimes lead to a confrontation. For many years since the foundation of the Irish State, the Catholic Church in Ireland told the politicians what to do; now the politicians are telling the church what to do. In Essay 5, I stated that the 'New Ireland' is a cold place for people of faith. We are living in an age of unbelief. Our enlightened atheists and humanists believe that religion is evil and none more so than Christianity and Islam. In Ireland, the big religion is Catholicism. About 80% of the population profess to be Catholics but not all are practising Catholics, in fact probably only about 40% are. About 7% belong to other religion, and 10% belong to the category No Religion.[1]

The basis of belief:

An interesting question is: Why do we believe what we believe? People believe all sorts of things. Some people believe that human existence is unreal and that what we perceive as reality is illusionary. Some people believe in ghosts, spirits, demons, djinn and the 'undead' that are abroad at Halloween and Samhain.[2] Many people believe in an Almighty God or Supreme Being that created and controls the universe and all things within it. Many people believe in the afterlife and places of eternal bliss or damnation that are called heaven or hell. Of course, 'educated' people and especially scientists, claim that all such beliefs are baseless and they call people of faith 'irrational' since all belief systems that are not based on scientific evidence are, in their view, invalid. They say that nobody has ever managed to produce a photograph of God and that what Moses saw in the Burning Bush was a mirage caused by the refraction of light from the sky by heated air in the desert. Simple minds had read divine intervention into natural phenomena. Now, in the modern age, God is dead and science is king. Atheists have been attempting to persuade everyone that religions really is 'the opium of the people,' quoting Marx and Nietzsche in support of their argument. They insist that nobody has ever managed to produce a single piece of hard evidence for the existence of God, or an angel, or a devil, or any other supernatural entity. Why then would any thinking person dare disbelieve such learned men who have demonstrated that science says there is no Supreme Being in outer space and there is no such thing as metaphysical reality. However, scientism is also a belief system and atheists are its prophets.

Of course, unbelief in an Almighty God is not a new phenomenon. It goes back to the Greek philosophers and was widespread across Europe in 18th and 19th centuries. More recently, modern atheists spearheaded by Richard Dawkins and the late Christopher Hitchens have been leading voices in the 'new atheism' that has great appeal for secularists, humanists and liberals. Debunking the existence of God and denouncing every belief system other than that of atheism has become very fashionable. However, in 2008 the apostles of atheism were upstaged by one of their own, a prominent atheist, Anthony Flew, who changed his mind and wrote a book entitled 'There is a God'.[3] That event shocked many devout atheists and the body that calls itself 'Atheist Ireland'.[4]

Many Catholics were dismayed when a Catholic parish priest, Fr. Joe Mac Donald[5] recently published a book listing five reasons why the

Irish Church deserves to die. Not everyone agrees with his analysis but a lot of practising Catholics take the view that the church deserves to be reformed. It needs to be reborn; some might say it needs to be converted to Christianity! The church at present seems to have little appeal for the younger generation. It is too set in its ways. Moreover, some of its clergy have been behaving badly and nobody can defend the horrendous issue of clerical sexual abuse. Fr. Mac Donald mentions the breath-taking arrogance of certain bishops; the fact that the church is male-dominated and women are kept down; the fact that is it is an abusive institution which has failed to deal with the problem of clerical abuse. He also mentions the fact that its hierarchic structure is top down and that it demonises and humiliates gay people. These are serious failings in a church that claims to be the true church founded by Christ. Christ did not exclude anyone. Not for the first time in its long history, the Catholic Church seems to have lost its way. Clearly, the church needs regular cleansing and we can see that Pope Francis is fully engaged in that undertaking, against dissenting voices in the Magisterium[6]. We should not forget that the church is a human institution and in every human institution there are bad apples. We all know about worldly and avaricious priests and power-hungry prelates. We know about the scandal of clerical abuse which was widespread and covered up. We know how the Church and State colluded in banishing 'fallen women' to institutional slavery in the Magdalene Laundries and Mother-and-Child Homes. The history of the Church has been less than edifying to say the least. It is disingenuous for the Church to pretend that so many horrible abuses were rare; they were widespread. The big question is how the Church is 'to restore all things in Christ' as set out by Pope Pius X in 1903. Clearly, it needs renewal but it must not give way to 'spiritual worldliness'.

Progressive Catholics:

Within the church there are traditional Catholics and 'progressive' Catholics. The so-called 'progressives' are immersed in secularism, humanism and modernism. They are at war with Christianity itself. They are uncomfortable with fundamental Christian dogma such as the supernatural, Sacred Scripture, biblical teaching on sin, salvation, etc. They deny the existence of hell. Thy say a loving God could not have created such an ungodly place. They say that all sexual relationships based on love are normal and legitimate and they have no problem with abortion, which they say is a woman's human right. On the other hand, traditional Catholics and Evangelical Christians believe that the Bible is the word of God and that the 'progressive' wing of the church is heretical, even Satanic. They say that the church has been infiltrated by false prophets, homosexuals, Freemasons and free thinkers. They are the ones who are responsible for the widespread moral corruption in the church. They are evil. Why would not Satan undermine the church from within? His trade is demonology. His foot soldiers are the so-called 'progressives' - the enemy within, the Antichrists in the church.

The Catholic Church in Ireland has come under sustained and vitriolic attack by secularists and 'progressive' Catholics over four main issues - abortion, same-sex marriage, clerical abuse and the mistreatment of 'fallen women.' The EU described Ireland's former ban on abortion was described as 'cruel' and 'unjust'. It also regards same-sex marriage as one of its many liberal tenets. Same-sex marriage is now legal in the Irish Republic even though the Church teaches that gay sex is sinful. I know that Christians do not disrespect gay people. However, I wince at the term 'same-sex marriage'.[7] I accept that nobody should be discriminated against because of their gender or their sexual orientation. However, I wish gay people would stop boasting about their gayness and trying to convert the rest of society to LGBT ideology. For me, the phrase 'same-sex marriage' is a nonsense.

It is against the law of God, against the order of nature, and linguistically, it is quite absurd. In every language in the world, marriage is defined as the formal union of a man and a woman. It is time to stop the bullshit, time to stop the language abuse. Future generations will refer to our time as the age of madness when secularists say that one's sexual orientation is a matter of personal choice.

Ireland was fiercely Catholic up to Catholic Emancipation (1829) and the Great Famine (1845-1852). However, during the period 1850 – 1970 the church leadership became too powerful and too doctrinaire. Several archbishops saw themselves as Old Testament prophets appointed by God to defend the forces of light against the forces of darkness. Three bishops in particular are now seen in retrospect as sectarian one-eyed prelates determined to extinguish both liberal and Protestant influence in Ireland. They are Cardinal Cullen, Archbishop of Dublin (1852-1878), John MacHale, Archbishop of Tuam (1834-1881) and John Charles McQuaid, Archbishop of Dublin (1940 -1972). Any politician or writer who dared to question the authority or teaching of the church got a 'belt of the crozier'. For instance, the writer John McGahern was dismissed from his post as a teacher following the publication of his novel 'The Dark' (1965) which was viewed by the church as pornographic. At that time, many prelates, Catholic and Protestant, were obsessed with sexual morality and eternal damnation.

The historical abuse of 'fallen women' during that dark period in Ireland cannot be brushed under the carpet. Space does not allow me to recount the horrors the Magdalene Laundries where unmarried mothers were imprisoned and treated like slaves. Many reports and books have been written about the Republic's institutions for 'fallen women' and the 'Mother-and-Baby Homes'

A nation's shame:

The final report of the Commission of Investigation into Mother-and-Baby Homes in Ireland (2021)[8] makes harrowing reading. The report covers the shocking treatment of unmarried mothers and their babies in 18 institutions (14 mother-and-baby homes and 4 county homes) from 1922 to 1998. There were 56,000 unmarried mothers and about 57,000 children in the homes investigated by the Commission. The saddest aspect of the report is the stifling and inhumane attitude of the Church, State and society that it uncovers towards unmarried mothers and their children not only in the early years of Independence but right up to modern times. The most shocking statistic of the report is the appalling level of mortality found among the children born in the institutes; 9,000 babies died of neglect, malnourishment and disease. It was wicked and inhumane but the shameful episode was ignored and condoned by the State, the Church and society for 76 years.

I shall not dwell on the shocking treatment meted out to the mothers and their children. The government left the matter in the hands of the local county councils, which were unwilling or unable to deal with the problem and they remained very much at arm's length. They simply passed the parcel to the Church, since there were no social welfare system available at that time. Then, in haste, mother-and-baby homes sprang up all over the country and nuns were ordered to run the homes and provide a refuge for the unwanted mothers and their babies. It was a blatant act of abandonment of duty by the government but now, some people are blaming the nuns for the fiasco. Certainly, the homes were no bed of roses for the inmates, but the local councils walked away from their obligation and paid the nuns a meagre capitation payment of £1 a week for each mother and child. The meagre payment did not go anywhere near the cost of providing sufficient staff, food, clothing, heating and medical care for mothers and their babies. It seems that many of the nuns reflected the puritanical Catholic ethos of period and looked down on unmarried mothers as unclean and unworthy. The same attitude also existed in Protestant families. Family honour and respectability were key values at that time and pregnancy outside of wedlock was considered shameful and sinful. All round, there was a profound lack of humanity, compassion and common decency. It is hard for people today to understand such indifference and such moral disdain for the unfortunate residents of the homes. Somebody should have told the nuns that there is no such thing as an 'illegitimate' child. All children are precious and legitimate no matter how and where they are born. All children have the same right to life and respect as the rest of us. And no mother should ever be condemned for giving birth; it should be a normal, natural and joyous event. The nuns blighted the lives of thousands of Irish women and their children. They have a lot to answer for; they allowed the malnourished children to die and it is said that they buried the dead in mass unmarked graves.

It is truly shocking that many mothers were subjected to disparaging comments and belittling remarks. What is utterly scandalous was the decision of the institutes to separate the mothers from their babies. They were treated as outcasts and made to undertake manual work for which they received no payment. They were virtual prisoners being punished for their sin. What was even more humiliating was the indifference of their own families to their plight. Society turned a blind eye to their wellbeing. The mothers were victims of systematic discrimination. Irish society was happy to disown and lock up their own errant daughters. However, the 'bad nuns' did not break into homes and kidnap the children. They were dumped on the nuns' doorstop because of family honour and respectability. In the eyes of the State and respectable society, the babies born out of wedlock were 'illegitimate' and hence unwanted in the family. The nuns were not blameless but at least they provided a refuge for the unfortunate women when their families provided no refuge or support at all. The women were destitute, abandoned by their family and had no option but to seek refuge in the local mother-and-baby home. It was Hobson's choice. At the end of a year in confinement, the mothers left while their babies were normally kept at the home up to age 5 for boys and 7 for girls. Some children were initially fostered and many were later adopted or sent to industrial schools.

Perhaps the worst punishment inflicted on the mothers was having to give up their babies for fostering or adoption. When adoption was legalised in 1953, many of the children were put up for adoption. Mother were, in some cases, persuaded to sign the adoption consent form. Many of the 'illegitimate' children were adopted by families in Ireland and 1,427 children were placed for adoption to the USA. The report states that there was no evidence of forced adoptions nor that large sums of money were paid to the institutes and agents in Ireland. It is obvious that the mothers suffered enormous emotional stress which never went away. They were torn and tormented by an enduring sense of loss, the trauma of separation and being forced to live with a sense of shame and stigma. Those poor women endured days of misery and nights of grief.

The Taoiseach, Micheál Martin, lost no time in making a formal State apology to the mothers-and-baby home survivors. It was, he said, a gross failure on the part of the State and Irish society, adding that it was a dark chapter in the history of Ireland. His words regarding blame were: 'We did this to ourselves as a society'. It was a case of society 'knowing but not knowing'. His apology and the government's admission of responsibility was welcomed by all concerned and it is hoped that the Commission's recommendations will be acted upon. It is good that the government has at last acknowledged the hurt and pain of the victims, empathised with their mental anguish and distress and agreed to reach out the hand of compassion and support. Three undertakings have been promised: (a) unfettered access to personal information regarding the birth record of the children, where possible with the consent of the mother, (b) a redress scheme for the surviving mothers, and (c) some financial contribution to be made by the religious orders which ran the homes on behalf of the State.

The report states that neither the Church nor the State obliged distressed young mothers to go to the homes. They simply ended up there because they had no other place to go. Not all the homes were equally uncaring. However, most of the homes were cold and harsh and did little to significantly reduce the children's prospects of survival. However, the cause of the high death rate was natural causes. The main cause of infant deaths was premature birth and malnutrition. The report notes that certain commentators put the high death rate down to marasmus (undernourishment) and lack of appropriate medical care. Many deaths seem to have resulted from prematurity, congenital debility, respiratory infections, gastroenteritis, tuberculosis. peritonitis, meningitis, spina bifida, heart disease and measles.

Most of the homes were cold bleak buildings which had no running water, heating, baths or indoor toilets. Much worse than the austere living conditions was the hostile environment created by the nuns who remained emotionally cold and distant. Especially shocking is the case of the 'Mother-and-Baby Home' run by the Bon Secours sisters from 1925-1961 at Tuam in County Galway. The remains of 796 babies were found in unmarked graves nearby, some in what one local resident claims to have been a septic tank. Mothers had to work in the home until their babies were adopted by families across Ireland, the US, Britain and Germany. It was a truly shocking that some 6,000 unwanted babies were given up for adoption.

Not all the homes were equally bleak and uncaring. The Regina Coeli hostel in Dublin, which was run by the Legion of Mary, admitted and cared for any and every pregnant mother needing refuge. Unlike the other homes, babies were not separated from their mothers. Instead, the staff supported unmarried mothers who wished to raise their child and made every effort to integrate them back into society. Records show that between 1930 and 1998, some 5,631 mothers and 5,434 children were admitted and cared for.

The Commission report by Justice Yvonne Murphy and her team is comprehensive, balanced and fair. It is truly shocking and should give us all reason to stand up for justice, human rights and equality of esteem. No woman deserves to be humiliated and punished for giving birth. The report has been criticised by certain sanctimonious socialists for not blaming the nuns, even suggesting criminal liability on their part. The report makes it clear that the bulk of the blame lies primarily with the State and with society in general, rather than with the nuns who operated the institutions. Obviously, the nuns were not blameless. They could have done more to keep mothers and their babies together and treat them with normal civility and respect. The church too could and should have raised funds for the welfare of the abandoned mothers but instead it chose to ignore them. In the end, it seems that no one body can be held responsible for the fiasco since everyone was complicit to a greater or lesser extent. The media, and especially 'liberal' politicians, feminists and RTE, will dwell on the blame game, but the real issue now is how best to atone for past wrongs and give the survivors not only an apology but redress and access to their birth records. The survivors have been denied justice for decades and have not been allowed to penetrate a wall of silence by the State and the institutions.

Moralistic morons:

The Irish Free State, which was established in 1921, undertook to honour the commitment of the 1916 patriots to 'cherishing all the children of nation equally'. However, it did exactly the opposite. It cast aside the whole spirit of justice, equality and esteem for thousands of its children and their mothers. A true republic seeks to protect the most vulnerable members of society. The Irish Free State, however, decided that unmarried mothers did not belong in the 'free Ireland'. They were unclean, immoral and had be removed from society and hidden behind a wall of silence.

They were outcasts in the eyes of the moralistic morons in the Free State. Their crime was that they were poor and pregnant. The State and society said in effect: 'Lock them up and tell the nuns to give them a hard time.' Now, in 2021, we are celebrating the birth of nation but we have little to celebrate since the State has defaulted on the basic human rights which are fundamental to the meaning of the word 'republic'. We are a republic in name only. The moralistic philistines have not gone away. They are still here, in government and in society. However, instead of preaching Victorian morality, they are now preaching liberal/secularist ideology. I refer to them as the one-eyed cyclopes – the so-called liberal politicians, the fake-news media, the disgruntled feminists and a raft of woke celebrities who echo the government's mantra of political correctness. The problem with cyclopes is that they insist that their view of reality should be shared by everyone. They get enraged and hurl rocks at anyone who does not share their destructive nature. We saw them in action on RTE's Sunday programme, 'The Week in Politics' (17 January, 2021) doing a hatchet job on the mother-and-baby homes Commission's report. Of course, in the 'New Ireland' only sanctimonious socialists and secularists get platformed on Irish media. The Commission's report is a scholarly work of research, based on data collected and analysed over five years and its tone and findings are objective and evidence-based.

As we read the Commission's report, we should not forget that the babies that died, died from natural causes – disease, malnutrition and lack of appropriate care. For the mothers and their babies, it was a sad case of dehumanisation that was allowed to persist for 76 years. One could even say that it was evil. However, it was nowhere as evil as the modern practice of human killing which was legalised by the Irish government in 2018. I am referring to the Abortion Act which terminated 6,666 innocent preborn babies in 2019. One wonders why the 'liberal' government and the media are silent on that mother of all scandals. Since 2018, we find ourselves living in a State where human killing is not only ignored but legalised. Those 6,666 preborn babies did not die of natural causes; they were intentionally terminated by the State. Let's call it for what it is, the mass murder of innocent unborn lives. One more, Irish society looked away, 'knowing but not knowing'. If the government had an ounce of humanity or moral integrity, it would repeal the Abortion Act forthwith, but it even refuses to consider the matter. The pro-abortion lobby in the Republic wants even more unborn babies killed by abortion. For instance, Amnesty International has announced that its main goal for 2021 is to legalise abortion in every country in the world. However, as a student of history, I know that one day those who engage in mass murder will he held to account by an international court. For me and for all people who uphold the right to life as the most fundamental of all human rights, that day cannot come soon enough.

Myopic liberals:

The doctrinaire stance of certain prelates on ethical issues is not found in the teaching of Jesus, in the 'Sermon on the Mount' and especially in the Golden Rule[9]: 'Do unto others as you would have them do unto you.' Senator Mullen (2020)[10] has reminded us that the values of equality, justice, concern for the poor and the common good do not stem from the Enlightenment or the French Revolution. They are rooted in Christianity. The idea of liberty as defined by John Stuart Mill and other rationalists is a paraphrase of the Christian injunction 'Do unto others...' The ethical principle is the same; we must not do harm to others - one person's freedom must not impinge on the freedom of any other person. That principle has been cast aside by the 'liberal' governments not only in Ireland but worldwide.

While myopic 'liberal' politicians in Leinster House love to kick the Catholic Church in the teeth at every turn, their woeful track record of not caring for the welfare of ordinary people does not seem to bother them in the least. They do not address the health and hospital crisis, the housing and homelessness crisis, the cost of living crisis, the public transport crisis, the mental health crisis and the rural Ireland crisis. For instance, children with scoliosis and other crippling conditions are left to wait for surgery for a year or more. Government ministers seem to have closed their eyes to human suffering on a grand scale in order to advance their 'liberal' agenda. They are quite happy for 'Focus Ireland', the 'Vincent de Paul Society', the 'Peter McVerry Trust' and other charities to look after the homeless and for the destitute and hungry to be fed by Brother Kevin and his staff at the 'Capuchin Day Centre', or by 'Corsscare', or at soup kitchens, as in the Great Famine. They do very little for the mentally ill but leave children and adolescents to languish in misery until they receive residential care in clinics run by the 'John of God Order', while those with suicidal ideation depend on the services provided by 'Pieta House'. We do not see our TDs and Senators on the front line. They sit on their fat backsides in the Oireachtas while people on low income sink into poverty. They seem blind to the fact that the streets of the cities and towns are awash with heroin, crack cocaine and cannabis. In our streets, we see open drug taking, robberies from person, home and shops, gun and knife crime, shooting and killing, sexual assault and racist thuggery. It is no longer safe to walk the streets of Irish towns and cities. People in rural areas are living in fear and dread of being set upon by criminal gangs. The government has shut down hundreds of rural police stations and given burglars free reign to loot and plunder, as the Viking did in ancient times. This is the 'New Ireland' that our liberal/secularist politicians have created. The same myopic politicians have the audacity to pontificate on the evils of religion and are constantly denouncing the Catholic Church for its teaching on social issues, such as abortion, sex education, moral formation, etc. They have closed their eyes to the murder and mayhem all around them. Crime has been steadily increasing under our 'liberal' dispensation. At present, somebody gets killed almost every day in Ireland but that is hardly surprising since the government has legalised human killing. When the government legalises the killing of unborn babies, why shouldn't the crime barons also have licence to kill? Murder is murder, no matter who does it.

Moral bankruptcy:

In the past, the church sometimes strayed from the path of righteousness. Obviously, it needs regular cleansing and renewal. We should not forget that Jesus was very critical of the elders of the old religion, who put on shows of piety and holiness. He referred to them as 'whited sepulchers' - righteous on the outside but full of hypocrisy and wickedness on the inside. He was not obsessed with the observance of the law. His focus was on purity of heart, on respect for every person, on love and kindness and forgiveness. His focus was not on doctrinal conformity but on moral living in freedom and justice. In a true republic, the government must be held to account by moral reason and not by appeals to historic sexual abuse or misogyny or homophobia by members of the Church. The problem at present in Ireland is that liberalism is not based on moral reason. It has no moral underpinning. Hence, the State should refrain from demonising the Church for the all the social ills that have resulted from the dogma of 'choice' that it preaches. According to the gospel of modern liberalism, people must be free to make their own moral choices. For instance, terminating an unwanted pregnancy is a woman's choice. Babies are now a matter of choice. Blasphemy is now a matter of individual choice. One's sexual orientation is a matter of choice; gay people are not born gay; they choose to be gay. Such logic has profound consequences for society which must be guided by moral principles. For people of faith, the moral code is the Ten Commandments and a firm belief that 'In God we live and move and have our being.' (Acts 17: 28). Liberalism is about living without God in the world. It is a morally bankrupt ideology. Its values are not based on moral norms but on humanist logic. It has no ethical sense.

False prophets:

In Matthew 7 we are told: 'Beware of false prophets. By their fruits you shall know them.' We should not be deceived by the false prophets of secularism, who proclaim that there is no evidence for the existence of God. If I were a theologian, I might be able to quote the five proofs of the existence of God as set out by St. Thomas Aquinas in his 'Summa Theologica.' In 'The God Delusion' Richard Dawkins argues against the 'five ways' but he mis-states them and shows an appalling ignorance of theology. He is a brilliant writer but his logic is all haywire. The 'delusion' he speaks of is all of his own making. A more rational discussion of the question can be found in Professor Nagasawa's book.[11]

There is no empirical evidence whatever that God does not exist. You can point to evil in the world and say that a merciful God could not have allowed it to happen. However, man has free will and everyone has to take responsibility for the choices they make. Obviously, Adam and Eve made a wrong choice. So did Cain. And so did thousands of evil people ever since. Scientism has a hard time disproving the existence of God. The scientific method has two ways of proving or disproving a hypothesis – the qualitative method or the quantitative method. I do not know of any evidence that would support the former while the latter is obviously self-refuting; if you choose to refute a null hypothesis which says: 'There is no God' you end up proving that God exists. Science is wonderful but there are large realms of truth that it cannot access at all, i.e. metaphysical reality. It cannot explain why anything exists.

Back to the Bible:

Why should a rational human being believe in the existence of an invisible God? If I were a philosopher, I might argue that it can be inferred by reasoning; there is no other possible explanation. However, I am not into ontological and cosmological evidence. I prefer to dwell on the material evidence for the Bible, which was written over 2,200 years ago by a number of inspired authors. We have abundant documentary and physical evidence for the Bible story. The Dead Sea Scrolls were discovered in a cave at Qumran some 13 miles east of Jerusalem. They include fragments of every book of the Old Testament, written in Hebrew and Aramaic during the period 200 BC to 68 AD. Over 15,000 biblical fragments and 500 manuscripts were found in that cave. Ireland is fortunate in that the Chester Beatty Library[12] in Dublin houses a priceless collection of biblical papyri, dating back from the 2nd to the 4th century A. D. including copies of the four gospels, the Acts of the Apostles, the letters of St. Paul and the Book of Revelation. No other event in human history has such a wealth of authentic documentary evidence. Textual experts have no reason to disprove the authenticity of the books of the Bible. Of course, the books of the Bible do not record history in the sense that history is understood today. Biblical exegesis is necessary in decoding the meaning of the texts and that varies on a scale from maximal to minimal interpretation. Biblical texts are a special genre and one must know how to decode them. Biblical exegesis requires a knowledge of the style and format of the sacred scriptures as well as a knowledge of Hebrew, Aramaic, Greek and Latin. Our English versions[13] were translated by biblical scholars. When you read the Bible, you are reading the most influential book that the world has ever known, and like all great book, it pays to read informed commentary on its origin, design, style, and its cultural impact on society. There are many such guidebooks to the Bible, for instance, Ryan & Tracey (2018).[14]

There is also the evidence of the spade. Archaeological excavations across the Near East from Ur in the Chaldees (in modern Iraq) to Mount Sinai validate the historicity of the events and places mentioned in the Bible. Archaeological evidence, when added to the evidence of the sacred scriptures, dispels the notion that the Bible is a fairy-tale. It is attested by copious documentary and physical evidence. The question which sceptics cannot answer is how the prophets from Aaron[15] to John the Baptist[16] correctly foretold the precise time, place and circumstance of the coming of the Messiah.

The 'little platoons':

In Essay 2 reference was made to Edmund Burke's 'little platoons'[17] by which he means the family, church and the local community. He says that the best life begins in the family. Family is the foundation of society. It is there that faith is implanted, nurtured and cultivated. When the family is broken, society suffers. We end up with a broken society and that seems to be happening in Ireland at present. In former times, families prayed together, went to church together, took part in parish activities together. In his book, 'Amoris Laetitia', Pope Frances[18] has noted that 'your children are as the shoots of an olive tree' (section 13); that the family is a place which is 'filled with the presence of God, common prayer and every blessing' (section 15); 'where parents become their children's first teachers (section 16) and later he speaks of the parish as 'a family of families'(section 87). And so we can conclude that Edmund Burke and Pope Francis are on the same page in stressing the vital role of good moral formation in the family and in the parish. And that explains why the Irish National schools were established as parish schools under church patronage but open to pupils of any religion or none.

Several of my friends are non-believers. They say that they do not want faith schools but they all send their children to the best Catholic or Protestant schools. They do not want Catholic hospitals but prefer to be treated at hospitals owned and run by Catholic nuns! Of course, they think that I am crazy to believe that the Bible is the word of God. They say that the Bible is a fairy-tale, no more than the demented ramblings of mystics wandering about in the torrid heat of the Middle East deserts. When I ask them which book of the Bible they find most objectionable, they are stumped. They have never read the Bible. They do not know that it is a collection of 73 books, 46 books of the Old Testament and 27 books of the New Testament. They tell me that the Irish Constitution needs reforming; that it was drafted by 'masterminds of the right.' However, they have never read the Constitution (1937) and when I read them passages from my copy, they walk away. When you argue against something, such as the Bible or faith schools or the Constitution, you should at least know what you are talking about! I am not a biblical scholar but at least I have read the Bible. For me, it is a holy book that should be treated with the greatest respect. I see no reason to profane the Bible nor places of worship. I see no reason to blaspheme the Almighty. I see no reason why people of faith should not be allowed to have their children educated in faith schools, all of which belong to the parish. I see no reason to refer to people of faith as 'irrational apes' which is insulting not only to humans but to apes. My 'liberal' friends insist that abortion is a woman's democratic right. They say that the decision to terminate a pregnancy is a woman's choice. They will not listen when I tell them that one's choices are limited; that choice has to stop when it impinges on another person's fundamental rights. They do not understand that the Constitution must uphold the principle of protecting all human life from the moment of conception to natural death. They tell me that such notions are old-fashioned.

People of faith believe that all human killing is immoral. They also believe that no normal woman wants to be the mother of a dead child - a child whose life she agreed to extinguish because the government told Irish women that they had the right of terminate the life of an unborn child if that was their choice. My friends only laugh when I quote Cicero, or the Bible, or Abraham Lincoln's words: 'No law can give me the right to do what is wrong.' They say that I am out of tune with modern 'progressive' thinking in the modern world of science and technology, which has nothing to do with Christian ideology. I understand their argument but I do not understand why they believe it to be the only authentic belief system. I merely point out that every coin has two sides. In the 'New Ireland' only one side is ever discussed - the secularist side. My essays speak of the other side that is erased from public discourse. My essays speak the unvarnished truth about a Republic that has lost all moral compass; it has become a republic as fake as the secularist ideology which is preached zealously by the government, by its many agencies, as well as by the secular media and especially by 'celebrities' who speak in fulsome terms of the new progressive liberal 'New Ireland' on RTE chat shows.

The Bible is the rock on which the Republic of Ireland was founded. It follows that the systematic removal of the Ten Commandments and the moral teaching of the Gospels from the Constitution by the false prophets of liberalism/secularism in the Oireachtas is a vile act of betrayal. Not for the first time in human history has a nation suppressed the faith and worshipped the golden calf. The republic was founded on the principle that 'in God we trust.' By voting for abortion and infanticide, for same-sex marriage and for blasphemy many Irish people have reversed the clock and said: 'In God, we trust NOT.' For many people, religion brings spiritual joy and peace of mind. Even the rituals of each religion enrich one's daily life. Little things like lighting a candle, saying a payer, pausing for a moment's reflection when the Angelus bell rings or reading the Bible make such a difference to one's life. Our whole live can be changed for the better if we learn to be at peace. We need to focus more on inner peace and the practice of stillness. As Andrew Norman (2010: 4) puts it 'we are constantly running away from ourselves, and we are thus unable to be at rest.'[19] People of faith can sleep in their bed at night knowing that they are predestined for eternal life - for an eternity of glory that is lasting and unchanging.

My point is that one cannot ignore religion. Moral considerations impact on everything we do. We know instinctively that some things are right or wrong. We may try to silence the voice of conscience but we cannot erase it. It is part of our genetic human endowment. All human life is constrained by moral order. People of faith believe that the moral order is universal. Christians, Jews and Muslims believe it is the word of God as revealed in sacred scripture and Catholics believe that is it codified in the moral theology of the Church.

The sad fact is that the faithful have been abandoned by many of the local pastors who have gone down the slippery road of liberalism and secularism. Bishops and priests are supposed to be holy men reminding the flock that our life here on earth is but a nanosecond on the eternity clock and that one day, perhaps sooner than expected, we will meet our Maker who will know whether we have lived by His Commandments. The Bible has very strong words to say about those who harm children or lead them astray. Jesus says: 'Whoever causes one of these little ones who believe in me to sin, it would be better for him that a millstone were hung around his neck and he was thrown into the sea.'[20]

Milton's great poem Lycidas (1638) speaks of the 'unfit shepherds' in the Church. Lines 122-127 read:

> What recks it then? What need they? They are sped;
> And when they list, their lean and flashy songs
> Grate on their scrannel pipes of wretched straw;
> The hungry sheep look up, and are not fed,
> But swol'n with wind, and the rank mist they draw,
> Rot inwardly and foul contagion spread.

Now, as in Milton's time, we hear the idle prattle of churchmen who spread 'foul contagion'. It will take an great moral awakening to take back the country from the godless within the church and from the vile gospel of secularism that the Irish government and its handmaids in the secular media are preaching and prescribing in the 'New Ireland'.

We, as a nation, would do well to step back in time and reread the wise words of people like John Henry Newman, who eloquently upheld belief in the harmony of faith and reason. He reminds us that we are all on a journey. We are all climbing a winding stairs to an upper room where we will find peace and rest. If we live by the Spirit we will experience inner peace. We must not listen to the false prophets who speak of 'bringing the Church up to date' - the liberal elite who want to rewrite the Bible and formulate a new 'progressive' religion or worse still, those 'liberal' politicians who wish to transform the Republic into a secularist state. Furthermore, we should know that there is always a price to pay for disobedience to God. I am confident that all will be well if we live under the wing of God's protection, as our founding fathers ordained in the Proclamation of the Republic, 1916.

In 1829, the Liberator, Daniel O'Connell won Catholic Emancipation for Ireland after centuries of Penal Laws and religious persecution under a foreign power. Now, more than ever, the Republic needs another Liberator to free the Republic from the enemy within - the peddlers of toxic secularism.

Endnotes:

1   According to the 2016 census, Catholics are 78.8% of the population, Other Religions 7.3%, No Religion 10%, No Stated Religion 4.8%

2   Samhain: An ancient Celtic festival celebrated by dancing and rituals on 1st November marking the beginning of winter.

3   Antony Flew (2008). 'There is a God'. London: HarperCollins

4   'Atheist Ireland': The name is pretentious since Ireland is not atheist. The correct name for that body of unbelievers in God is 'Atheists of Ireland'. A typical example of language abuse

5   Fr. Joe McDonald (2017). 'Why the Irish Church Deserves to Die'. Dublin: Columba Books

6   Magisterium: The teaching authority of the Catholic Church

7   Dr. Gerard J.M. Van Den Aardweg (2015). 'Science says NO: The Gay Marriage Deception'. Lumen Fidei Press.

8   Final Report of the Commission of Investigation into Mother and Baby Homes, 12 January 2021. The Executive Summary (76 pages) and the full report (2,865 pages) may be downloaded at www.gov.ie

9   The Golden Rule in Matthew 7:12. The ethic of reciprocity is found in most religions and cultures.

10   Senator Ronan Mullen. The Irish Times 24.11.2020

11   Yujin Nagasawa (2011). 'The Existence of God: a philosophical introduction'. London: Routledge

12   David Hutchinson Edgar (2003). 'Treasuring the Word: An Introduction to Biblical Manuscripts in the Chester Beatty Library'. Dublin: Town House

13   The most famous English translation of the Bible is the King James (1611) version, which is the approved Protestant version. However, many later versions in modern English have replaced it. The Catholic Bible contains seven books called the Apocrypha, which other versions omit. A popular English version is the Douay-Rheims Bible, which is an accurate translation of the St. Jerome's Latin Vulgate Bible.

14   Salvador Ryan & Liam M. S Tracey (2018). 'The Cultural Reception of the Bible'. Dublin: Four Courts Press

15   Aaron was a prophet, high priest and brother of Moses during the 14th century BC.

16   John the Baptist was the last of the prophets.

17   'the little platoons': Edmund Burke (1790). 'Reflections on the Revolution in France'. Modern UK edition (1987) by J.G.A. Pocock. Indianapolis: Hackett Publishing Co. The metaphor of the 'little platoons' refers to families working together in harmony in the local community, getting things done by collaborative enterprise. It is an old concept in rural Ireland, known as 'meitheal' (team work) – neighbours coming together at harvest time, turf cutting, etc

18   Pope Frances (2016). Amoris Laeititia. (The Joy of Love). Veritas. (Sections, 13, 15, 87)

19   Andrew Norman (2010). Learn to be at Peace. Oxford: Fairacres Publications. p.4

20   Mark 9.4

7

THE LEGALISATION
OF ABORTION

And they shall have no pity on the fruit of the womb;
their eyes shall not spare children. (Isaiah 13:18)

What is the most important topic that nobody is talking about in Ireland today? In fact, it is a topic that nobody in Europe seems willing to talk about. Of course, I am referring to the legalisation of human killing. In 2019, the Irish State 'terminated' 6,666 unborn Irish lives and in 2020, a further 6,577 Irish lives were terminated. Not only is that act of barbarism not talked about, the 'liberal' government regards abortion as the great step forward. Clearly, killing unwanted unborn life is normal practice across the UK and the EU and the Republic must fall into line or be regarded as backward. People must know that the mass murder of innocent human life is not a new idea. It has a long history. And just as nobody talked about human killing in Germany under the Nazi regime, nobody talks about it in Ireland today. It is the will of the people, just as the Holocaust was the will of the people in Germany. We are evolving as liberal human beings and old ideas such as the ban on taking human life is no longer relevant in the modern age. Some old-fashioned people of faith, especially Christians, Jews and Muslims say that abortion is the murder machine of our time but we live in a parliamentary democracy and we have to be 'progressive' and

81

allow people to walk away from the taboos imposed by religion. That is the narrative one gets from the Irish government, the media and secularists.

The Republic of Ireland is a parliamentary democracy. However, in recent years, its claim to representative democracy has become more illusionary than real. Professor A. C. Grayling (2017)[1] has spoken and written about the modern phenomenon of the subversion of modern democracies by dark money, corporate power, social media, populism and falsely designed referenda. Governments know very well that their survival depends on public support and public opinion can and must be shaped by those in power. In the late nineteenth century, a British historian, Lord Acton, remarked: 'Power tends to corrupt, and absolute power corrupts absolutely. Great men are always bad men.' In other words, a ruler's sense of morality lessens as his power increases. That saying seems to be borne out in the case of many so-called democracies in our time. A classic example of the abuse of power here in Ireland is manner in which the Irish government managed to persuade the electorate to vote for abortion. In January 2018, the Taoiseach Leo Varadkar announced that due to popular demand, the government intended to repeal the 8th Amendment to the Constitution and replace it with a provision enabling the Oireachtas to legislate for abortion. From a liberal/secularist perspective, it was essential to undo a fundamental principle in the Irish Constitution, namely the right to life. The 8th Amendment to the Constitution outlawed abortion and made it a criminal offence. In his speech, the Taoiseach painted the 8th Amendment as a major roadblock to the health and wellbeing of Irish women who were forced to go abroad in order to obtain an abortion. Of course, he made no mention of the unborn child's right to life nor the fact that legalising abortion implied turning a blind eye to the intentional killing of a human life.

Nothing shows the demise of democracy and moral responsibility by the Oireachtas more than the manner in which abortion was legalised in 2018, an event that I have described in my monograph on the issue.[2]

The legalisation of abortion, more than any other measure, stands out as a masterclass in parliamentary abuse of power. It was, like several other Constitutional 'reforms' seen as liberating Irish people from the tyranny of the Church and in particular of the Catholic Church. According to 'liberal' ideology, the Irish State has to be cleansed of its traditional faith-based culture by tearing up the original Constitution and replacing it with new secularist norms which would legalise every form of depravity known to man, including human killing, divorce, same-sex marriage, blasphemy, the banning of moral formation in faith schools, the denial of freedom of conscience and the banning of peaceful protest. Over the past thirty years, the Irish State has lost all pretence of being a true republic and it has become a sham republic. Representative democracy is the hallmark of a true republic but democracy cannot work if political leaders lie every day and conduct business underhand in an assembly where representative democracy and moral responsibility have gone out the window. The transformation of Christian Ireland into a liberal/secularist state had its origin in two sources, one external and the other internal. Across Europe, modern liberalism has spread its wings and the old Christian Europe has been almost wiped off the map. EU member states that still hold on to their traditional Christian principles and culture are deemed backward and people of faith are regarded as irrational. The ideology of the EU is liberal, secularist and progressive - all very loaded terms in the cultural lexicon of liberal democracy. When an independent republic surrenders its national sovereignty to an external parliament in Brussels, it must be willing to accept a paradigm shift in ideology, culture and socio-political thinking. It must fall into line with the norms, laws and governance of the Supreme Oracle of power which we call the European Union. As regards change from within the Republic, socio-political sentiment has also changed fundamentally. Discontent and disillusion with the ideals and mores of the existing Republic had been simmering for decades. Writers and intellectuals felt that the 'terrible beauty' which W.B. Yeats had written about had withered. They felt that the Republic had become a theocratic state and that Catholic bishops were telling the government what to do think especially on social, cultural and educational matters. Women wanted parity of esteem with men and feminists wanted more than tokenism; they wanted real power and a seat at the top table. Even devout Catholics began questioning the faith in which they were raised and its teaching on such matters as divorce, abortion, homosexuality, moral formation, sexual freedom and family planning. In addition, the air reeked of the foul contagion arising from the scandal of clerical sexual abuse, the brutal abuse of boys in industrial schools, the detention of 'fallen women' in the Magdalene Laundries and the horrific scandal of the Mother-and-Baby Homes. It could be said that the Republic was ripe for re-invention.

Constitutional chaos:

The abortion issue cannot be looked at in isolation from the Constitutional crisis which surrounds it. We know that the Constitution of Ireland 1937, which replaced the Constitution of the Irish Free State 1922, is still the Constitution of the Irish Republic even though it has been amended 32 times which means that that the original Constitution has been virtually torn up. Articles 40 to 44 set out the fundamental rights of permanent residents in the Republic. However, fundamental rights are not absolute and all Constitutional laws may be amended by means of a referendum. The original Constitution specifically recognised and protected the right to life in Article 40.4. The right to life refers to one's natural life span from the moment of conception to natural death. It is a fundamental right in every constitution since it is based on Natural Law which is the cornerstone of all jurisprudence. However, an explicit ban on abortion is not normally contained in the Constitution but it may be outlawed under the provisions of the Criminal code. In 1983 a pro-life amendment – the 8th Amendment – was inserted into the Irish Constitution which pro-abortion journalists have described as a remarkable coup by right-wing Catholic conservatives![3] They would say that, wouldn't they! I shall not dwell on the rights and wrongs of that particular amendment which proved to be very divisive socially and politically. It is sheer humbug to claim, as feminists do, that it puts women's lives are at risk unless they have access to abortion. Professor Eamonn McGuinness – former president of the Institute of Obstetrics and Gynaecology – has stated that 'The Eight Amendment' has one medical effect only: it prevents Irish doctors, as an elective matter, causing the death of an unborn child.'[4] For 35 years, it protected thousands of unborn but unwanted babies from being 'terminated'.

When you want the change socio-political climate of a republic, you begin by removing from the Constitution any measures that run counter to your ideology; in other words you remove certain fundamental rights and entitlements enshrined in the Constitution. The Irish government in power in 2018 knew very well that it would require enormous skill, cunning and persuasion in order to convince the electorate to consent to something as gross as human killing and especially the deliberate killing of an innocent unborn child. In order to manipulate the electorate into voting for abortion, the government knew it would have to resort to the Machiavellian principle that deceit is a politician's best weapon. There was no way a Christian county like Ireland was going to vote for mass-murder. Therefore, abortion would have to be promoted and sold under a different label and described as a much needed and positive outcome not just for pregnant mothers but for any female over 15 year of age who wished to terminate an unwanted pregnancy. We do not know who came up with the idea of putting the abortion issue to a referendum; not just an ordinary referendum but a cleverly designed referendum which did not even mention the dreaded word 'abortion.' Somebody in the Cabinet obviously decided to stand democracy on its head by inventing a rationale for something which was obviously morally repugnant but politically expedient. All that was needed was the opening up of a Pandora's box of dirty tricks designed to present abortion not as human killing but as a health issue for women. Then a battery of 'experts' would roll into town to (a) sing the praises of abortion and (b) to silence the 'tumult' of the pro-life opposition and demonise the pro-life movement. The first step in the process of brainwashing was articulating a rationale for the proposed Constitutional change. Popular consent did not fall from heaven; it had to be engineered. In May 2018 Irish people voted in a referendum to allow the Oireachtas to legalise abortion. The Pro-abortion side won the referendum and celebrated in a manner reminiscent of the Storming of the Bastille. The Abortion Act, called the Health (Regulation of Termination of Pregnancy) Act was signed into law on 20 December 2018. As a result, the revised Constitution no longer protects the right to life. That right has been erased from the current Constitution and a new Article (Article 40.3.3) states: 'Provision may be made by law for the regulation of termination of pregnancy.' The government seems proud of the fact 6,666 unborn babies were intentionally 'terminated' in 2019 and 6,577 in 2020.

I am sure that future generations will look back on the mass-killing of Irish unborn babies in 2019 and 2020 as the most inhumane and barbaric episode in Irish history since the Great Famine. The manner in which abortion was legalised will be forever remembered as the deceit of the century. At this point I should rest my case. The Republic is truly dead. The legalisation of human killing was the final nail in the coffin of the Republic. Other evil acts were also enacted, in particular the legalisation of same-sex marriage and the de-criminalisation of blasphemy. I certainly do not approve of blasphemy but those who blaspheme will sooner or later meet their Maker and will have to have to answer for their wickedness. However, I would strongly advise the former Minister of Justice, who felt passionately that Irish people should be free to blaspheme, not to speak about his support for blasphemy on his next trip to Saudi Arabia, or the Gulf States, or Iran, or Afghanistan, or South East Asia, or North Africa or Nigeria or East Africa. As they say in Zanzibar: 'Dead men do not blaspheme!' My ideology is obviously different from his. My ideology is human rights and for me the right to life is by far the most precious and important human right. It is obvious if you do not have the right to life, you cannot possibly have any other right.

The rationale for abortion:

It was easy for the government to create the case for abortion since it had long been a burning issue with feminists, socialists, liberals and secularists. All that was necessary was to invoke the mythology concerning abortion that had been festering over thirty years. That rationale is based on a whole raft of myths which are too many to be discussed here. I shall deal briefly with three of the main myths, all of which are equally inane yet they are trotted out with great frequency by the government and the media. They are (a) the myth that abortion is necessary for the good health and welfare of women, (b) the myth which denies the humanity of the foetus, and (c) the argument that abortion is a woman's human right.

a. The first myth concerns the life-saving argument for abortion which asserts that the 8th Amendment (1983) put women's lives at risk, citing the tragic case of Savita Halappanavar who died in 2012 supposedly because she did not have access to abortion. However, three separate inquiries into the cause of her death found that she had died of sepsis which had not been detected and treated. Clearly, the life-saving argument for abortion flies in the face of objective medical evidence. However, the government decided that the case for abortion could be camouflaged under the cover of 'good health' and it planned to shift the focus from killing the unborn child to protecting the mother's pregnancy. It was, of course, a blatant deceit but, as we know, a lie which is frequently repeated is often perceived as truth. The Minister for Health, Simon Harris, by some extraordinary twist of logic, somehow convinced himself and his colleagues in government that the killing of unwanted unborn babies was necessary for the health of pregnant mothers. He obviously did not do his homework. The medical research evidence for abortion is virtually non-existent. For example, a large-scale survey of 5,650 women who had taken the abortion pill was conducted by Professor Abigail Aiken at the University of Texas. Only 1.5% of the respondents cited health concerns for wanting an abortion. Moreover, it is also obvious that Mr. Harris is profoundly ignorant of the immediate and long-lasting harmful health consequences of abortion, such as blood clots, bleeding, severe pain or cramps, weakness and especially increased risk of breast cancer. The link between abortion and breast cancer is still being evaluated by medical experts.

Some 50 international medical studies show that many women who had an induced abortion develop breast cancer. However, I am not a doctor and I cannot possibly know the precise link between abortion and breast cancer. I do know, however, that the claim made by the Taoiseach, that abortion in the Republic would be 'safe' and 'rare' was completely spurious. It certainly was not 'safe' or 'rare' for the 13,243 unborn babies that were 'terminated' in 2019 and 2020. Furthermore, Mr. Harris and his team, who drafted the Abortion Bill, obviously chose to ignore the well-documented and long-lasting mental trauma and regret that women who consented to have their unborn baby aborted. Several longitudinal studies show that such women suffer severe regret, guilt feelings, depression, insomnia, suicidal tendency and alcohol abuse.

My opinion on medical matters does not count. I am not a medical expert. However, it is instructive to read what Irish experts have to say on the matter. Four leading obstetricians and gynaecologists in Ireland - Professor Bonnar (Trinity College Dublin), Professor O'Driscoll (University College

Dublin), Professor O'Dwyer (University College Galway) and Professor Vaughan have affirmed that there are no medical circumstances justifying direct abortion. That is also the view of several other medical experts, such as Professor McGuinness (former president of the Institute of Obstetrics and Gynaecology) and many other healthcare professionals. Hence, the argument for abortion on health grounds is totally baseless. It is obvious that abortion is NOT healthcare.

b. The second myth is even more absurd than the first. It asserts that the foetus in not human. Abortionists refer to the foetus as some sort of pre-natal entity that becomes a human being only at birth. I shall not waste space on discussing the humanity of the foetus since it is a biological fact. Advances in 4D ultrasound technology show clearly that the foetus is not just 'a clump of cells'. It is an emerging human child. In Gaelic, the foetus is known as 'beo gan breith' (alive but not born). It is a living human being and the life of every living human being must be protected in law. What is really astonishing in the Irish context is the decision of the Joint Oireachtas Committee to propose that unrestricted abortion should be legalised during the first 12 weeks of pregnancy. You do not have to be a gynaecologist to know that gestational age is irrelevant to the abortion debate. It is just as repugnant to kill a human life in the first week of pregnancy as in the final week. And it does not matter whether the killing is done by medical or surgical intervention. Arguments based on the staging or methodology of abortion are totally irrelevant and fallacious.

c. The third myth concerns human rights law. It asserts that the ban on abortion in the Constitution is a denial of a woman's human rights. The claim here is based on the notion of 'bodily integrity' which supposedly gives a woman the 'right to choose' whether to give birth or terminate her unborn child if she so wishes. She may decide to opt for abortion for any number of reasons if she decides that the pregnancy is unwanted. However, babies are not choices. The emerging baby in the womb is not part of the woman. The pre-born baby is a living being, with its own unique DNA, heartbeat, brain waves and blood type. The 'bodily integrity' view ignores the fact that there are two bodies, two distinct lives. The right to life of the unborn child is just as precious as the right to life of any other human being. Hence, it is clearly understood that human killing is never a matter of choice; it is repugnant to natural law, to moral law and to constitutional law. The pro-abortion slogan 'My Body, My Choice' is utterly vacuous.

Feminists in the Republic claimed that the 8th Amendment to the Constitution banning abortion was incompatible with human rights. Professor William Binchy - Ireland's most eminent Constitutional and human rights lawyer - has refuted that myth in several papers which are available on the Internet. The repeated claim by the abortion lobby that abortion is a human right is utterly false. There is no right to abortion under any international law, covenant or treaty. On the contrary, the inalienable right human right – the right to life, is enshrined in international law. The UN Convention on the Rights of the Child states that 'every child has an inherent right to life' (Article 6) and in the preamble it states that 'the child, by reason of his physical and mental immaturity, needs special safeguards and care, including appropriate legal protection, BEFORE as well as AFTER birth.' In a civilised state, the law must protect the life, health and dignity of all children, both born and unborn. In June 2021, the EU parliament declared abortion access a human right. However, the resolution is non-binding on member states and has been rejected by many. The bottom line is: Killing babies, born or unborn, is NOT a human right. It is wrong to intentionally destroy unborn human life. Any person who cares about human rights will insist that abortion and infanticide are criminal acts that no human law can claim to legitimise. Furthermore, the Rights of the Child should be legally protected in the Constitution.

However, since the articles of the Constitution may be amended by a referendum, it seems necessary to make some of them plenary (i.e. absolute). I would like to see a plenary power in the Constitution along the following lines: 'All Children, born or unborn, have an inherent right to life from the moment of conception to natural death.' Such a provision is mandated in the UN Convention of the Rights of the Child. I am sure that our constitutional lawyers could frame such a plenary power to be included in our Constitution if Irish people (and not politicians) wanted legal protection for those who have no voice - the unborn.

Sociologists tell us that abortion always existed in the past and will always exist in the future because some women will always have to face the reality of a crisis pregnancy. However, they conveniently overlook the fact that abortion entails the taking of a human life and that is something that no civilised state can tolerate much less legalise. In a true republic, every life is protected in law and no life is less precious than any other life. There are two victims in every abortion. First and foremost, there is the innocent unseen victim – the unborn and unwanted child who is 'terminated'. The second victim is the mother. No woman wants to be the mother a dead child. Perhaps she may have been influenced by the repeated slogan of feminists about 'bodily integrity' i.e. that every woman has a moral right to decide what to do with her body. Perhaps she believes that the World Health Organisation is right in recommending abortion in order to reduce the problem of global over-population. Beside, terminating human beings is not a new idea. For centuries, during the slave trade, black lives did not matter. During the Nazi regime in Germany, Jewish lives did not matter. During the Great Famine in Ireland, 'popish' lives did not matter. In our time, unborn human life does not matter. We have to accept that abortion is legalised murder. It is the murder machine of our time. We know that is so, but we pretend not to know. The Irish psyche is very good at 'knowing but not knowing.'

We all understand that women may have a genuine reason for wanting an abortion. It may be due to financial difficulties, social pressure and fear, not the right time, or a diagnosed fatal foetal abnormality. However, it is seldom due to concern for the mother's health. That is the fake rationale that the government and feminists use to justify access to abortion. They excel at the art of euphemism. The phrase 'abortion care' must rank as the greatest euphemism in the English language. The intentional taking of human life is now regularly described as 'abortion care' by the HSE and the media.

A false referendum:

Apart from inventing a false rationale for a 'liberal abortion regime' to be put to the people in a referendum on the Repeal of the 8th Amendment in May 2018, the design of the referendum is a prime example of how the political will of the Oireachtas can override the will of the people. I am saying that the referendum itself and the government's subsequent actions based on it, amounted to a coup. Firstly, the wording of the referendum proposal was deliberately ambiguous. People were asked to vote YES or NO to repeal of the 8th Amendment but the voting paper added in small print the following stipulation: 'Provision may be made by law for the regulation of termination of pregnancy'. It seems that the electorate did not read the small print carefully. The wording here was blatantly misleading. Pregnancy is terminated when the child is born but in this context the phrase 'termination of pregnancy' is a euphemism for 'abortion'. That phrase was a deliberate distortion designed to deceive the electorate. It asked the electorate to give the government a blank cheque to legalise abortion without mentioning the word 'abortion'. Instead, it used the phrase 'termination of pregnancy' to mean the deliberate and intentional ending of an unborn human life. There is a world of difference between direct abortion and the case where a foetus dies as an indirect result of a medical procedure which was necessary to save the life of the mother. Under the principle of double effect, it has always been the position of the State that it is morally permissible for a doctor to perform necessary medical procedures in cases in which the mother is almost certain to die without the procedure, for instance, an ectopic pregnancy or aggressive uterine cancer. In such cases the word 'terminate' is inappropriate since the death of the embryo or foetus is an unintended side effect. In plain language if you 'terminate a pregnancy' you kill a human child before he or she sees the light of day. The government and the media are no longer using the term 'abortion' and now call it 'reproductive rights'. No thought whatsoever is mentioned for the rights of the child in the womb.

Secondly, the legalisation of abortion may be seen as setting a legal precedent for human killing. If it is legal to kill a human being at the beginning of life, why not also legalise the killing of human beings at the end of life? Where does one draw line? Terminators are in the business of killing. Nobody was therefore surprised when a Bill came before the Dáil in October 2020 seeking to legalise euthanasia. Of course, it did not mention the ugly word 'euthanasia' just as the referendum in 2018 did not mention the ugly word 'abortion', instead it resorted to the old trickery of euphemism, calling the proposed Bill 'Dying with Dignity'. Irish politician excel at the abuse of language but it seems that most Irish people are not good at decoding it. They obviously did not reflect on the unintended consequences of giving the Oireachtas the power of life and death. The most fundamental of all human rights is the right to life. No person, no law and no government can extinguish that right. If the right to life is removed from the Constitution, all other human rights become meaningless. A state which does not protect all human life is no longer a true republic. A true republic must 'cherish all the children of the nation equally.' In the 'New Ireland', however, human life is now a woman's choice. Such terms as the 'termination of pregnancy', 'the right to choose', 'reproductive rights,' 'abortion care' and 'a liberal abortion regime' are the weasel words that are used to blur the meaning of the sheer awfulness of abortion.

It is obvious that all human life must be protected in law. If life at its beginning is not protected in law, none of us is safe. Medical science tells us that life begins at conception. It follows that abortion is a direct attack on life.

What was utterly bizarre was the manner in which the result of the referendum on the 8th Amendment was announced in the upper square of Dublin Castle before a cheering crowd of pro-abortionists, including government ministers who were dancing and cheering as if Ireland had won the World Cup. Of course, the outcome was never in doubt. All the big gun were on the pro-abortions side – all the political parties barring a handful of honest TDs and Senators, all the media, especially RTE and The Irish Times, plus the illegal funding of the Irish Family Planning Association (IFPA), the Abortion Rights Campaign and Amnesty funded by George Soros's 'Open Society Foundation' and the active support of other state-funded bodies such as the National Women's Council of Ireland (NWCI) and the Irish Human Rights and Equality Commission (IHREC). The Pro-Life side was barred from the media, received no funding whatever and women harmed by abortion were not allowed to tell their story. It was a victory for propaganda, brainwashing and deceit of the most vile kind in a State where real democracy is subverted by lies, big money and gross abuse of the parliamentary system. It was Irish politicians and not the people who legalised human killing. Their action in this and many other similar cases is ample proof that the idea and ideals of a true republic have been extinguished in the 'New Ireland.'

The Citizens' Assembly

Before looking at the Abortion Bill (2018), it is important to review the mechanisms that the government used to justify the legalisation of wide-ranging abortion. The Irish government is very good at creating popular consent by devious means. In 2017, it outsourced consideration of some of the most controversial issues in society to an outside body called a 'Citizens' Assembly'. It is a totally bogus body, unelected and incompetent to advise the government on key political issues which members of parliament are elected to deal with. That body consists of 99 citizens supposedly randomly selected to represent the views of the common people. Of course, every dog on the street knows very well that the so-called 'Citizens' Assembly' was created specifically as a means of shaping public opinion. For instance, in the case of the repeal of the 8th Amendment to the Constitution, removing the ban on abortion, most of the 'expert witnesses' invited to speak on the subject were pro-abortion advocacy groups such as Amnesty Ireland, the Irish Family Planning Association, the National Women's Council of Ireland as well as left-wing politicians. In addition, several so-called medical experts were invited to explain why women supposedly need abortion for health reasons. I would have grave reservations about the objectivity of 'experts' such as Dr. Peter Thompson (NHS England), Dr. Patricia Lohr (British Pregnancy Advisory Service) and Dr. Gilda Sedagh (Guttmacher Institute, N.Y.) To call them 'natural expert witnesses' is an abuse of language. The Chair did not explain who invited those pro-abortion 'experts' or why. Furthermore, it was agreed that advocacy groups would not be invited. However, a whole raft of pro-abortion groups attended and were allowed to explain to the members why abortion was necessary for various reasons. They included Colm O'Gorman (Amnesty International), Dr. C. Henchion (Irish Family Planning Association), Orla O'Connor (National Women's Council of Ireland) and several other pro-abortion advocacy groups.

The Assembly did not address the core issue at all, namely, the ethical question of the protection of foetal life. It side-lined so many issues that it lost all credibility. Nobody wanted to see the elephant in the room — the unborn child. Why was the question of human killing not on the agenda? Obviously, the aim of the Assembly was to invent a rationale for the deliberate killing of unwanted unborn babies. Only depraved people would have taken part in such an inhumane exercise.

The Chair, in her final report, claims that the Assembly was 'an exercise in deliberative democracy' and that the 99 members who were selected are 'a representative sample of ordinary members of Irish society.' Nothing could be further from the truth. A stratified random sample of 99 is far too small to represent the views of the entire adult population of the Republic. It is impossible to generalise from such a small sample. Ten counties were not represented at the Assembly. Furthermore, from a statistical viewpoint, the randomness of the sample was compromised by the non-attendance and non-response of members. When a large number of the sample is not included, the whole process is corrupted. The final report of the Assembly states that membership at each session varied from 72 to 92. Not one of the ballots on each issue was voted on by the whole sample. That glaring error seems to have eluded the Chair.

The government's master plan was to create a rationale for abortion by means of a bogus 'Citizens' Assembly' and then have its recommendations refined and ratified by a joint Oireachtas Committee. The players in both 'gatherings' did not realize that on a matter of life and death, farce has no place. It makes a mockery of our political system. The Citizens' Assembly was an obvious farce but a greater farce was to follow when its aberrant recommendations were forwarded to a joint Oireachtas Committee for official approval and endorsement.

The Joint Oireachtas Committee:

Oireachtas Committees form a key part of our so-called democratic republic. Parliamentary Committees in a normal democracy look at issues in a fair and dispassionate manner, duly considering both sides of the issue under consideration and allowing members to see and hear all the relevant evidence. Its terms of reference are clearly defined in a book of Standing Orders which stipulate the composition of the committee, the role and responsibilities of the chair, the calling of expert witnesses, the hearing of testimonies, the rules that insure that members do not stray beyond their remit and above all else the absolute requirement for equality of membership on both sided of the matter under discussion. No such decorum applies in the Oireachtas and it most certainly did not when its members debated the abortion issue.

The Oireachtas Committee consisted of 20 cross-party TDs and Senators under Senator Noone (chair) – an outspoken pro-abortion member of government. It met weekly over a period from 4 April to 20 December 2017. It was directed to approve the recommendations proposed by the Citizens' Assembly. Needless to say, the whole proceedings were even more farcical than that of the Citizens' Assembly. Its members worked on the principle that if you pack the jury with false witnesses, you will get the desired outcome. Its profound bias is obvious in its allocation of 'expert witnesses'. There were 24 invited speakers known for their strong advocacy of abortion and only 4 pro-life speakers. Like the Citizens' Assembly, it failed to address the core issue, namely the intentional termination of foetal life and it endorsed the government's liberal policy of giving women the right to terminate the life of the unborn if that was their choice. Killing an unwanted foetus was down to a woman's choice. Of course, the TDs and Senators on the Joint Oireachtas Committee did not mention the horrid word 'abortion' at all, nor did it appear in the Abortion Bill which followed. They preferred the euphemism 'termination of pregnancy' overlooking the fact that the debate was supposedly about protecting the right to life, which is the most fundamental right in every Constitution in the world. One cannot call a State a republic if it legalises human killing and especially the killing of its most vulnerable members, the unborn. We all know what 'terminators' do. We should not forget King Herod, nor Mr. Hitler, nor Pol Pot, nor Oliver Cromwell, all of whom were expert at terminating unwanted people. We should not forget that the practice of 'terminating' unwanted human beings led to the Holocaust. It is reasonable to ask who will be next on the 'termination' list if we kill babies before they see the light of day. If the State has the power to terminate one class of unwanted human beings, i.e. unborn babies, why would it not have the power to kill any other class of unwanted persons such as frail older people and individuals with significant disability.

We should not forget that the Oireachtas endorsed the findings of the Citizens' Assembly without questioning or testing their validity. The members acted like a researcher who sets out his or her conclusion on page one of their thesis, before stating the hypothesis, or the rationale behind it, before collecting valid and relevant data, or analysing the data according to strict criteria, checking the validating process and finally arriving at a finding based on the evidence. It was the TDs and Senators who legalised the intentional killing of unborn babies in 2018 and some members of parliament felt that their abortion proposals were too restrictive and should be revised to legalise abortion on demand. Of course, the Irish people did not vote for mass murder. It was the Joint Oireachtas Committee that persuaded the government to enact wide-ranging abortion. What is truly amazing is the findings of the Committee had already been agreed before deliberations on the issue even started. One member, Deputy O'Connell, openly admitted that the issue was already pre-determined when she declared on day one of the hearings that 'We are all abortionists in this room'.[5] The pro-abortion faction in government created a smokescreen around the abortion issue and as a result many honest TDs and Senators who voted for abortion, failed to see through the smoke.

The manner in which abortion was legalised in Ireland will one day be seen as the deceit of the century. Propaganda changed public opinion; the Citizen's Assembly created the rationale for abortion; the Joint Oireachtas ratified the recommendations of the Citizen's Assembly and finally the government changed the law. As a result, human killing is now legal in the

Republic of Ireland. Of course, some abortionists still deny the humanity of the foetus even though no serious biologist in the world believes that nonsense. Somebody should have told the members of the Oireachtas that life begins at conception. And somebody should have told the Supreme Court that human rights do not begin at birth. However, the Supreme Court is supreme in legal matters and its ruling cannot be challenged. I suspect that the learned judges know that the Ciceronian principle of Natural Law is the cornerstone of all jurisprudence.[6] Their ruling that human rights begin at birth is like the offside ruling in football. It is always right even when it is wrong!

I shall not discuss the 'hard cases' that arise in debating the abortion issue since it is a hotly contested medical matter. My focus is on protecting human rights and I simply repeat the basic democratic principle in every true republic and in every civilized society that every human being has the right to life and no committee, no assembly and no government has the right to terminate a human life. The word 'terminate' must never be used in the context of human life. The proposal to 'terminate' unborn human life speaks volumes for the corrupt system of government that pretends to be a democratic republic.

The final report of the Joint Oireachtas Committee on the proceeding is as false as the process itself. However, the minority report by Deputy Fitzpatrick, Deputy McGrath and Senator Mullen summarises its design, scope and work quite aptly in its title: 'An unacceptably flawed process has led inevitably to cruel and unjust recommendations.' The report is available online.[7] For a good review of the incredible bias inherent in the remit and findings of the Joint Oireachtas Committee see Cora Sherlock (2017).[8]

The Health (Regulation of Termination of Pregnancy) Act 2018:

The final act in the great deceit was 'The Health (Regulation of Termination of Pregnancy) Act 2018' which was enacted following the drafting and passing of the 'Termination of Pregnancy Bill'. I have already pointed out that the wording of the referendum proposal ('Provision may be made by law for the regulation of termination of pregnancy.') was grossly misleading in that it failed to convey the legal effect of repealing the 8th Amendment. The proper proposal which was not put to the people should have been: 'Should members of the Oireachtas have the right to legalise abortion?' I am convinced that such a proposal would have been rejected out of hand. No mature Irish person would have allowed a biased secularist/liberal regime to decide that it was legal to 'terminate' unborn human life.

The most extraordinary thing about the Abortion Bill is the fact that it is riddled with ambiguity and abuse of language. In legal discourse, words and terms have very precise meanings but the Abortion Bill abounds in lexical and semantic confusion. To begin with, it is wrongly named the 'Health (Regulation of Termination of Pregnancy) Bill 2018'. It is not a 'Health' Bill at all. It has nothing to do with healthcare. It is about legalising abortion but the word 'abortion' is nowhere mentioned in the Bill. Section 9, which deals with the risk to life or health, states that a termination may be carried out where two medical practitioners, having examined the pregnant woman are of 'reasonable opinion' that the foetus has not reached 'viability'. It goes on to say that one of the medical practitioners must be an obstetrician and the other an 'appropriate medical practitioner'. The phrase 'reasonable opinion' is so vague as to be meaningless. What makes an opinion 'reasonable'? Surely ending a person's life requires absolute certainty and not mere opinion! According to many medical experts it is virtually impossible to determine 'viability' with any degree of certainty. What exactly is an 'appropriate medical practitioner'? Is it somebody in a money-making abortion clinic?

The legalisation of abortion is a classic case study in mendacity. The government lied about everything, including the name of the Abortion Bill. They lied about freedom of conscience for doctors and healthcare workers opposed to abortion. The Minister for Health made numerous outlandish claims. For him, the term 'freedom of conscience' means if a GP is not willing to kill the unborn, he or she must get somebody else to do it. He lied about the 'ample' scrutiny of the Bill before it was published in October 2018. Instead of dealing with the multiple crises in his dysfunctional Department, he was running around like a headless chicken, tweeting almost daily about his great scheme for the liberation of Irish women and acting like a little pharaoh in squashing all opposition to his abortion scheme. It seems that the important question as to who would carry out the 'termination' service on behalf of the government was treated as an afterthought. Somebody obviously decided that it would have to be the GPs even though they had not been consulted on the matter. To win them over to a scheme which plainly ran counter to the Hippocratic oath taken by doctors, it was agreed to pay then a generous fee of €450 for each medical abortion consultation they would undertake. Very few GPs signed up to the government's Faustian deal.

The Abortion Bill was fast-tracked through parliament even though the government promised that there would be 'ample' time after the referendum to scrutinise any proposed legislation. However, the Health Minister point blank refused all amendments to his 'Health Bill' as it made it way on to the statute books. I shall not deal with the shocking inhumane aspects of the Bill which have been described elsewhere as 'the most unjust and inhumane ever to come before the Dáil.'[9] However, I fail to understand how the Health Minister showed such perverse intransigence and profound inhumanity regarding amendments to his Bill. A total of 180 amendments were tabled but not one of them was conceded. His 'Health Bill' (sic) ignored the concerns of GPs, nurses, midwives and pharmacists over conscientious objection as set out in their 'Code of Professional Conduct and Ethics'. The amendments are too many to list here, the most striking being the following:

- its refusal to allow conscientious objection by doctors and health workers.

- its refusal to provide pain relief for the unborn in late-term abortions. In Ireland, pain relief is mandatory whenever animals are slaughtered. Unwanted unborn babies, however, are denied any sedation.

- its refusal to outlaw abortion on grounds of gender or disability.

- its requirement that any baby which survived a botched abortion must be left to die since that was the mother's intention.

- its refusal to ensure that the remains of aborted babies are disposed of in a dignified manner according the wishes of the parents.

- its refusal to require parental permission for a teenage girl seeking a medical abortion.

I cannot understand why Irish people gave the government permission to terminate unwanted unborn babies. For me, no baby is unwanted. Every baby is gift from God and a reason to rejoice. Anyone who cares about human rights knows very well that all human life is precious from the moment of conception to natural death. I fail to understand how any thinking person would vote for human killing. What I find most curious is the fact that respectable journalists failed to see the elephant in the room – the unborn child who is 'terminated'. For me there is absolutely no circumstance that can justify the taking of human life. All human life must be protected in law. I am sure that every mother knows very well that abortion is wrong. They know instinctively what is right and wrong. They are the victims of abortion culture. The real criminals are those in the abortion industry – those who promote and practice abortion.

Space does not allow me to deal with several anomalies around the abortion issue, in particular, the following:

- Advising mothers to dispose of the unborn child by flushing the 'pregnancy remains' down the toilet.

- Allowing late-term abortions
- Refusing to allow sedation for the victim in late-term abortions
- Legalising feticide whereby the unborn baby is given a lethal injection into the heart.
- The use of aborted foetal cell use in vaccines
- The use of aborted body parts in medical research. No normal human being can ever agree to the sale or use of body parts for medical, scientific, or commercial purposes.

The Abortion Act (2018) is the most horrendous piece of legislation on the Irish statute books. I do not know of any other republic in the world that refuses to allow amendments to its proposed legislation and more alarmingly, I shall never get my head around the willingness of Irish politicians to normalise and legalise the intentional killing of human life. The Abortion Act 2018 has proved beyond all doubt that the Ireland is no longer a true republic.

Many doctors in Ireland regard abortion as morally reprehensible. You should read a recent study in the British Journal of Obstetrics and Gynaecology (BJOC)[10] based on interviews with doctors carrying out abortions in Ireland. Some of the doctors interviewed describe the abortion procedure as 'brutal' and 'awful'. They talk about their 'internal conflict' and their 'emotionally difficult' feelings at 'stabbing the baby in the heart'. One of the doctors confessed to getting sick in the corridor afterwards because of the sheer awfulness of the procedure. However, in the same study, some of the pro-abortion doctors interviewed express no regret over terminating babes with a 'fatal foetal abnormality'. They need to go back to medical school to learn about such matters. They are only concerned over the possible threat of litigation arising from ending human life. We know that at least one perfectly healthy baby was wrongly diagnosed as having a fatal foetal condition and was terminated at the National Maternity Hospital in Dublin. We do not know how many babies have been wrongly diagnosed as being non-viable. Such information is not disclosed.

The argument that is missing at the moment is that all human life, whether born or unborn, is sacrosanct. In a true republic all life matters. In a true republic nobody gets killed. In a true republic all the children of the nation are cherished equally. The right to life is absolute, hence, we must all save life, save civilisation, save our soul – the soul of the nation and each person's soul. A true republic must uphold the fundamental principles of civility, truth and equality of esteem for all human life. Sadly, the Republic of Ireland no longer protects the norms of democracy. It has normalised the abnormal and it has legalised human killing. The ruling 'liberal' elite has created a deeply divided nation and we know very well from history that a nation which is divided against itself cannot stand. The Republic at present is in chaos politically, socially and morally. I say this with regret because I know that most Irish people agree that no government, no institution, and no person may terminate a human life. Every normal Irish person knows that human killing is a crime against humanity. Their mistake was giving the Oireachtas the power of life and death. It was 'liberal' politicians, the secular media and fake feminists who manufactured the rationale for abortion and it was the Oireachtas which, by devious means, legalised wide-ranging abortion.

The gravest problem in Ireland at present is the deliberate killing of pre-born lives – the lives of innocent but unwanted human beings. It is a scandal that politicians, the media and many ordinary citizens have chosen to ignore, just as many German citizens ignored the Holocaust. All other problems pale into insignificance compared to the intentional taking of human life. For me, it is utterly bizarre, but I am an alien in the 'New Ireland'. I find it incomprehensible that the massacre of the innocents is not only ignored but it is condoned and fully endorsed by the government, the media and a whole raft of fake feminists who regard the taking of human life as their 'choice'.

The Bible contains 13 verses about the taking of human life.[11] Those who promote and practise human killing will be held to account. The

Biblical injunction 'Thou shalt not kill' applies to all human life, including preborn life. All human life is precious in the eyes of God.

Before I formed you in the womb I knew you,
and before you were born I consecrated you. (Jeremiah, 1:5)

Respect for human life is a sacred concept in all world religions, not only Christianity, but also in Judaism, Islam, Buddhism, Hinduism, etc. Human killing impinges on the whole person. It affects the heart as well as the mind. The deliberate killing of a human child, either before or after birth, is an act of barbarism. For a scholarly analysis of Article 40.3.3 and the abortion issue in Ireland, see Jennifer Schweppe et al.(2008).[12]

In conclusion, I repeat the simple fact that many Irish people have chosen to ignore the simple fact that abortion is the murder machine of our time. The Proclamation of the Republic at Easter 1916 states that a fundamental right of every Irish person is the right to life, 'cherishing all the children of the nation equally.' The legalisation of abortion means that the Irish state is unworthy to be called a republic.

Endnotes:

1   A. C. Grayling (2017). Democracy and its Crisis. Oneworld Publications
2   James M. Bourke (2019). Reflections on the Abortion Issue in Ireland. Lumen Fidei Press
3   See Emily O'Reilly (1992). Masterminds of the Right. Dublin: Attic Press; also Rosanna Cooney (2018). 'Story of the 8th: How right-wing Catholic groups staged a remarkable political coup. On JOE 22.5.2018.
4   Professor Eamon McGuinness. The Irish Times, 6 April, 2018.
5   The Irish Times, 19 October, 2017
6   Cicero: De Legibus, Book 3 and De Re Publica, Book 3
7   Google.com: Minority Report. 29 December 2917
8   Cora Sherlock (2017). 'Shambolic Oireachtas Committee on the 8th Amendment reduced to a kangaroo court.' Catholic Voice, 3 December 2017

9   For a detailed analysis of the Abortion Bill 2018 see the *Life Institute* website at the following address: https://thelifeinstitute.net/news/2018/analysis-of-the-abortion-bill

10   Jonathon van Maren (2020). 'Patriots: The Untold Story of Ireland's Pro-Life Movement'. Life Cycle Books
     BJOG, 2020 Sep 15,doi:10.1111/1471-0528.16502

11   Bible verses: See Exodus 20:13, Proverbs 6: 16-19, Matthew 15:19, Romans 13.9 and Revelation 21.8

12   Jennifer Schweppe (editor) (2008). 'The Unborn Child, Article 40.3.3 and Abortion in Ireland'. Dublin: The Liffey Press.

8

EDUCATION AS
INDOCTRINATION

I sometimes ask teachers and lecturers a simple question: What is the goal of education? The answers I get generally focus on the transmission of the knowledge and skills that young people need to survive in the information age. In other words, the old transmission paradigm still lives - education is seen as a preparation for life in the modern digital world. It has to be utilitarian and instrumental. However, in faith schools (Catholic, Protestant, Muslim, Jewish) one gets a different response. There, education is seen as much more than book learning and the transmission of skills. They adopt a holistic approach, which is about forming the whole person and establishing moral values. The great majority of Primary schools in Ireland are parish schools, 96% under Catholic patronage. Until recent times it is fair to say that the driving force behind Catholic schools and colleges was the holistic model based on the Newman's idea of raising children within a specific ethos or moral climate which permeates every aspect of the school day. However, one cannot fail to notice the hostility to Catholic faith that many members of parliament have been articulating. Their anti-Catholic prejudice is stunning. For instance, in a Dáil debate in June 2017, Deputy Bríd Smith called for the Catholic Church to be put 'in the dustbin of history where it belongs.' She and her colleagues on the left are role models of hate speech. They are regular panellists on

RTE chat shows and are much admired by the 'liberal' media. They are especially venomous over the fact that most of the National Schools in the Republic are under church patronage. They are not State schools. They are parish schools, built on church land and funded in part by the church membership. Catholic parents want their children to be educated in a Catholic ethos, and Protestant parents, Jewish parents and Muslim parents want the same right. The choice of school is guaranteed in in the Constitution. Article 42·4 states that the State shall provide free primary education and that it must have due regard for the rights of parents in the matter of religion and moral formation. However, many secularist members of government want to stamp out all moral formation in Primary and Post-primary schools. They like to blame the church for many of the social ills in society instead of accepting that such ills are due entirely to the government's gross incompetence and disinterest. Naturally, a liberal / secularist government will do its utmost to infect the educational system with its toxic ideology. I shall presently outline how it does this by reforming the curriculum, making it more 'modern', i.e. more secularist. Nobody objects to people of a non-religious persuasion having access to secular schooling for their children but they should do what faith schools have done, namely, put their hand in the pocket and contribute to the building and maintenance of their secular schools. Schools are not funded by the government; they are funded by the taxpayers.

The ethos question:

In my area of Dublin, there are several excellent faith schools serving the Catholic and Protestant population. There is also a Jewish school and a very large Muslim school nearby. The parents here are happy to have their faith respected and their children educated in their particular religious ethos. Of course, those schools accept students of other religions, as well as students of no religion, who are not required to attend the period set aside for Religious Instruction. Will the government listen to the wishes of parents on this important matter? Of course, not. The 'little pharaohs' in the Department of Education are determined to phase out the particular ethos of faith-based schools which are state-funded. Of course, educational indoctrination is not unique to Ireland. It happen whenever democratic voices are silenced by xenophobic rulers. Ireland has always had its fair share of such people, not only in government but also in the church.

The best teachers:

One of the good things about the Republic of Ireland is that it has always had very good teachers, schools, colleges of Further Education and universities. The training of Primary school teachers has been outstanding and we are fortunate to have the best Primary school teachers in Europe. They are familiar with the child's stages of cognitive development as described by Piaget and they know how to move pupils on from the 'concrete operational' stage at upper primary to the 'formal operational' stage at secondary level. They are also familiar with Bruner's ideas about discovery learning and the concept of the 'scaffolding of learning' which is necessary for learners to uncover new knowledge. Good teaching is, therefore, defined as maximising learner engagement. However, at Upper Secondary level the focus of teaching changes dramatically especially in form 5 and 6 when students take on the serious business of preparing for a high-stakes school leaving examination and the need to achieve the highest possible grades and points required for entry to a university or college of further education. Good teaching is then re-defined as that which gets the best examination results. Teachers have to cover a very demanding curriculum and they naturally 'teach to the test'. At this level, education becomes a bucket-filling process – filling the head with all sorts of useless information about English literature, French grammar, trigonometry, calculus and quadratic equations. I often wonder why Euclid's obsession with the isosceles triangle and Pythagoras' obsession with the square on the hypotenuse are of such vital importance to Irish students. I am still struggling go forget all the useless stuff that I leaner in my boarding school and I am astonished at what teachers did not tell us at school. We learned very little about the universe, about astrophysics, about the rise and fall of the great civilizations, about archaeology, about the human brain, about philosophy, about psychology, about linguistics. Like most of my classmates. I managed to pass my Leaving Certificate with honours in six subjects but I left school quite ignorant of many branches of knowledge. However, it was not all a waste of time. In my primary school, we learned how to read and write, to how do 'parsing and analysis,' how to spell tricky words like 'cygnet' and how write a well-formed sentence. Ever since then I have been interested in educating myself and helping to educate others. The most important lesson that I learned first at home and later at school was that truth matters, 'To thine own self be true' was written in large print above the blackboard. It was many years later that I discovered the origin of those wise words, namely 'Hamlet' (Act 1, Sc.3). At that time, everyone subscribed to the notion that truth matters but in the 'New Ireland' neither our secularist journalists, nor our 'liberal' politicians nor the national broadcaster, RTE have taken Polonius's words to heart. For them, truth is what you want it to be.

College students:

'Liberal' education is about individual freedom and personal choice. In the 'New Ireland', the 'Me Generation' is all about me, my choices, my human rights, my body and my entitlement to be myself. My choices are all that matter even when they impinge on 'your choices'. College students call themselves 'normal people' living in a fun-loving society in which the prevailing social norms must give way to counter-culture. Normal people break all the conventional rules with impunity and boast of their drunken binges, their weekend raves and their sexual adventures. It is none of my business what people behind closed doors. There is obviously a time and a place for loving relationships but please do not bore me with your bragging about your loutish behaviour and your sexual adventures on television chat shows or write about them in obscene books such as J. P. Dunleavy's (1955) 'The Ginger Man'. For me, college education is much more than a romp through four years of loafing and fornicating. In former times, it was about 'feeding the mind' and helping students to unlock the meaning of life and enabling them to discover their own truth. One read the great thinkers - Plato, Aristotle, Plutarch, Cicero, St. Jerome, Thomas Aquinas, etc. University life was a great intellectual journey across the world of classical scholarship and it was also a journey of discovery inside oneself. One discovered that every branch of knowledge is a system of systems whether it be religion, language, science, music, etc. and it took great mental probing to uncover the rules that govern and regulate all those system networks. However, we do not live in one dimension and it takes a lot of time and effort to grasp metaphysical reality, which some scientists dismiss as mythology but which nonetheless has concerned philosophers since the dawn of time. I am referring to the ultimate questions about the meaning of life, the nature of reality, and belief systems. It seems to me that education today is about the inculcation of liberal norms rather than seeking objective truth in a world of subjective interpretation.

The problem of knowing:

The old debate about the acquisition of knowledge goes back to the great Greek philosophers and it became a burning issue in Europe in the 17th century. Rene Descartes (1637) held that knowledge comes only through the application of pure reason. Hence his view is called rationalism. It is a belief in innate ideas, reason and induction which he encapsulated in the phrase 'Cogito, ergo sum' (I think, therefore I am) meaning whatever thinks, must exist. That view has been the foundation of cognitive science, strongly supported by modern scholarship, for instance, Chomsky's view that language is made in the mind and by modern mathematics and physics. John Locke (1692) however, held the opposite view. He held that when born, the mind of the child is a 'tabula rasa' (empty slate) to be later filled with data derived from sensory experience, hence the empiricist dictum 'Nihil est in intellectu, quod non prius fuerit in sensu.' (There is nothing in the intellect which was not first in the senses.)

The transmission model:

Education is a key concern of government and it is rightly considered a human right in the Constitution of most democratic states. However, there is some confusion over the exact purpose, scope and nature of the most effective pedagogy. There are two fundamentally different approaches. The first, for want of a better name, is known as traditional epistemics. It is also known as the deductive model or the a posteriori[1] model. In this model the teacher is seen as the fount and source of all knowledge and the learners are seen as empty vessels, recipients of the master's great knowledge, which has been acquired by long observation and experience. You can visualise this model as the great guru standing on his soapbox and proclaiming:

> Now you must know
> That this is so.

Here the favoured pedagogy is rote learning based on the old Skinnerian behaviourist model of stimulus → response → reinforcement, which in the classroom translates into Presentation → Practice → Production. The main focus is on choral repetition with the teacher's booming voice intoning the famous words: 'Repeat after me'. Pupils repeat the prescribed response until they are blue in the face. The knowledge thus acquired is later regurgitated in progress tests and an end-of-year examination. A robot would love such a system of learning.

The creative construction model:

The second model is known as revolutionary epistemics[2] or the inductive model or the a priori model. The approach is based on cognitive science Here things are very different. It is a learner-centred approach. Its focus is on engaging learners in the learning process and the teacher's role is to facilitate learning by providing the necessary 'scaffolding' to nudge learners in the right direction so that they, working co-operatively in small groups, can uncover new information. Here learning is seen as a creative construction process and the motto is:

> If you can see what I can see,
> Then perhaps we can agree.

The idea here was well expressed by Plutarch[3] who famously said: 'Education is not a pail to be filled but a fire to be lighted.' In the creative / constructive approach leaners go out into the forest, gather the firewood, make the fire and use its light to dispel darkness. It is obvious that the inductive model is more stimulating for the learners since they are in the driving seat. They learn a lot from each other and they become very good at problem-solving, sharing ideas and expressing their views. Most importantly, they never forget knowledge that they discover by and for themselves. The main drawback is that it is hard to organise such learner-centred and task-based learning in very large classes of 20 or more. The inducive model goes from specific examples or input to a general rule or pattern. The focus here is on the process. The older deductive model does the opposite. It goes from the general rule to specific examples which are presented by the teacher and practised by the class often by rote learning, chanting or reading aloud. The focus here is on the product.

Cultural indoctrination:

Why am I dwelling on this matter, you may ask. My concern is that when the Department of Education sees its mission as indoctrinating students in its particular ideology and hence it will obviously prefer the deductive approach. The content and methodology of education is prescribed in the new, revised curriculum, which de-emphasises moral formation and seeks to remove the particular ethos that faith schools wish to preserve. We have all heard about the Machiavellian exploits of Ruairi Quinn who served as Minister for Education from 2011 to 2014. As a devout socialist on behalf of the Labour party, he sought to liberate Ireland from the tyranny of the Catholic Church. He railed against Church patronage of Primary schools in the Republic and launched the 'Forum on Patronage and Pluralism' in April 2011 to transform faith schools into secular schools, ignoring the fact that 96% of Primary schools in the Republic are parish schools, built on church land owned by the Catholic Church and the Church of Ireland. Then, although parents were not even consulted, he appointed a number of 'lesser pharaohs' to oversee the work of the Forum. They do not seem to realize that the Government of Ireland does not provide Primary education; it provides FOR Primary education; it grant aids others to do it on the State's behalf.

Liberal governments are good at erasing history. Mr. Quinn will be forever remembered as the Education Minister who decided to erase the teaching of history from the Junior Certificate curriculum. Once more, acting as a 'little dictator' he decided that the past is best forgotten and without any consultation with stakeholders (teachers, parents and pupils) he ordered that history be removed from the curriculum. Somebody should have told him that the past is never past. History is the story of a nation and it is the property of all its people. History is not something that happened a long time ago. We are shaped by our history. We are all, to some extent, victims of our history. It has left deep scars that may take a very long time to heal. We have to go back in time in order to discover ourselves and our culture. We do not have to live in the past but neither should we deny it. Our history is all around us, in the very air we breathe, not only in our history books but also in the hills and valleys, in our lore and literature, in our art and architecture, in our song and poetry. We are links in an unbroken chain. We receive from the past and hand it on to the future.

RSE brainwashing:

The Department of Education has recently launched a brainwashing programme to erase moral formation from the school curriculum. Its 'little pharaohs' detest the concept of moral formation and the religious ethos of faith schools. Less than 10% of Irish people claim to belong to the category of 'no religion' but in the 'New Ireland' it is the secularist minority that now has control of educational policy. The concept of popular consent has been thrown overboard by the devout secularists. In their zeal to brainwash the youth of Ireland, they have added a new subject to curriculum called 'Relationship and Sexuality education' (RSE). It was launched in all Primary and Post-Primary schools in September 2020. Its stated goal is to ensure that all children from junior infants upwards receive 'objective sex education' with the goal of embedding sexual awareness in children's social development. Of course, we all know what the word 'objective' means in the lexicon of secularism. Its real purpose is to indoctrinate children with a secularist view of human sexuality by explicit instruction on the following topics:

- Relationships and sexuality
- Belonging and integrating

- Sexual consent
- Friendship and its expression
- Emotional health
- Contraception
- Abortion
- Masturbation
- Same-sex marriage
- Safe sex
- Substance use
- LGBT relationships

On paper, the RSE programmes looks like the mass-indoctrination programme that is currently being implemented by China on Muslims in the Xinjiang Province.[4] The Irish version of RSE is seen by many as a programme of indoctrination designed to normalise sexual practices that are not only against the law of God but also against the order of nature. However, the government sees RSE as necessary behavioural modification in the shaping of the liberal 'New Ireland'. I do not know who gave the bone-headed 'little pharaohs' in the Department of Education the right to impose such a programme on all state-funded Primary and Post Primary schools in the Republic. However, it soon became apparent that RSE would face serious difficulties in faith schools, especially those under Catholic patronage. Then, fearing electoral wipe out, the government reluctantly conceded that schools were free to deliver RSE according to their religious ethos. Faith school then gave a mighty sigh of relief. They were free to do as much or as little RSE as they thought fit and it could be delivered through the existing Religious Instruction classes. It is not for me to say how RSE is to be integrated into Religious Instruction especially in a run-away curriculum which needs more time for new subjects such as environmental studies and digital technology. I think that RSE is too narrow in scope. It should not focus so narrowly on sex education. Sex education is neither moral nor immoral; it is part of human biology.

However, it also has a moral dimension and the moral formation of pupils is the core ethos of faith schools.

Certainly, at Primary school level, children need to be told how to protect their innocence, how to respond to sexual abuse in the home, school or society, how to respect the opposite sex and how not to outrage the modesty of others. They must learn to walk away from bad company, especially those who engage in homophobic name-calling and bullying. All of those matters need attending to and were previously included in the invisible curriculum called 'good manners'. In upper Primary classes, some faith schools have handed over RSE to Catholic agencies, such 'Accord', 'Pure in Heart', and 'Youth Defence' which do excellent work which has nothing to do with corrupting young minds. I am aware of the challenges in delivering moral formation in Catholic schools, as outlined by Eugene Duffy et al (2012)[5] and I know that many parents would prefer if sacramental preparation was done by the church outside of normal school hours. I think that RSE is a subset of moral formation and that the main focus of all education should address such issues as racism, bigotry, respect for all people and for all belief systems, etiquette and good manners. My point is that it is vitally important to deepen the connection between moral formation and moral living. If we want a just society, we must first have just people. I fail to understand why pupils at Primary school level need systematic instruction in sexual behaviour. Of course, it is deemed an essential component of 'liberal' education. 'Our culture has done its damnedest to reduce sexual relations to a recreational activity, with no constraints other than consent and age-appropriateness.'[6]

At Post-Primary, Years 1-3, some colleges are using a textbook entitled 'On Track: Direction in Your Life' which is an excellent guidebook since we all need direction in our lives. Most of us muddled our way through adolescence. Teenagers clearly need direction in making the transition to adulthood and if RSE helps in that regard, it clearly serves a much needed purpose. A glaring weakness in our education system is its failure to equip teenagers with essential life skills such as the following: good health and diet, personal healthcare, dress sense, social skills and manners, domestic skills, financial discipline, language awareness and communication skills, behavioural skills, coping with emotions and stress and problem-solving family issues instead of engaging in open rebellion.

Higher education:

In Ireland, the higher education goes, the worse it gets. Ireland's universities used to be among the best in the world, especially Trinity College Dublin (TCD)[7] and University College Dublin (UCD)[8]. They were what Newman - who founded the Catholic University, now UCD - called 'seats of learning'. But that was long ago when Irish people wanted and received a holistic education. That was before the dumbing down of education began. Now, it seems to me, many Irish universities and tertiary institutes are merely 'jam pot' factories, turning our industry-ready graduates, who have never read the classics, or philosophy, or linguistics or any other form of education that broadens the mind. Even the lecturers have lost the plot. They can no longer say what the role of a university is. Before COVID struck, students would attend mass lectures, were given assignments to do, were told where to find relevant data and off they went to their laptops to find and download useful information from the Internet, which they paraphrased, re-packaged and submitted in an attractive folder. No more tutorials, no more informal discussions with fellow students in the 'square', no more mentoring by supervisors. Now, due to COVID almost all lectures are online with minimal face-to-face contact with lecturers; a new approach called 'blended learning' is the norm. A robot could do well in this new age of information technology and machine learning. It is a matter of pressing the right buttons. But college student are not robots. Mass lectures are for morons and any fool can download online data and research. Students need to have a dialogue with their lecturers and professors; they need the freedom to ask questions, not only about the course content but also the ultimate questions about the meaning of life. Education must inspire students to ask questions, to seek enlightenment, to grow in wisdom. Students should examine the social, cultural and religious parameters, find out what the great philosophers had to say on various issues, uncover the rules by which things are governed, - the rules of science, logic, mathematics, linguistics. Real education should be an inductive problem-solving process, a developmental process, which changes people, making them wiser, more conscious of themselves and their environment and helping them to learn how to learn. Sadly, higher education at present seems obsessed with market economics. I am not saying that students do not master course content in their chosen discipline and I am not saying that university lecturers are cretins. What I am saying is that there is too much focus on the science of getting rich. The purpose of higher education in Republic today seems to be fixated on 'earning' rather than 'learning'. Let me state my thesis loud and clear: The end product of all education is the cultivation of WISDOM. It would be wonderful if we had a Minister of Higher Education who understood that concept!

The pursuit of wisdom has to be raised to the top of the educational agenda. Without wisdom, our world will lapse into barbarism. When one looks at the appalling state of the world today - regional wars, terrorism, poverty, famine, crime, corruption in high places, abuse of power - one has to ask: Where is the wisdom? All of this is my preamble to the work of the most profound of educationalists, John Henry Newman,[9] who in his seminal lectures in Dublin, 'The Idea of a University' (1858) tells us clearly what the goal of university education should be. He says the role of a university should be the cultivation of wisdom. Its mission is not at all utilitarian, namely preparing young men and women for the job market. Is it not odd that it took a Catholic priest (and a former Anglican) to remind us what higher education is about? His sanity is stunning. Let me recap the gist of his thesis. First and foremost, a university must be 'a seat of learning'.

It should aim at producing generalists rather than narrow specialists. It must focus on providing a liberal education, i.e. knowledge for its own sake. It must make the cultivation of wisdom its primary objective. In other words, it must produce thinking individuals. After all, our species is called Homo sapiens. Hence, any kind of knowledge is its own reward. A university must enable students to seek knowledge for its own sake and no other end beyond itself. Above all else, it must help students to think and especially to think critically.

Today Newman's ideas are no longer held in esteem even in the university that he founded. Irish universities are very good at professional training but they need to do more to than skill-getting and job training. Space does not allow me to say how Newman's ideas might be implemented in our modern world of digital technology. I agree that students should have access to a university if that is their wish. However, not everyone needs a university education. Those seeking a good professional qualification might be better off in a third-level college. There are currently 25 such colleges in the Irish Republic, offering professional training, many of them enjoying high global status. There are nine public universities, which can hardly be called 'seats of learning'. The Higher Education Authority needs to redefine the role of a university and ensure that it is more than a job-training institute.

Obviously, a proper university must ensure that all of its lecturers are experts in their chosen discipline and not mere political appointees. There can be no compromise on this matter. They should be appointed on academic merit alone and not on grounds of gender or ethnicity or any other criterion. All dead wood needs to be removed. And, quite frankly, there is a lot of dead wood around. Only one Irish university, Trinity College Dublin, currently makes it close to the top 100 in world rankings. However, given adequate funding, there is no reason why all nine Irish universities should not make the top 100 world ranking.[10] One thing is clear; Irish universities are not doing enough to broaden the mind and cultivate critical thinking. A republic worthy of the name deserves outstanding scholarship but it seems to me that some of our universities are offering courses designed to promote a particular ideology. It is not clear to me how Women's Studies or Gender Studies can be regarded as academically rigorous disciplines. Do not women's rights come within the domain of Law and Sociology? I cannot speak for all the Irish universities but I know that behind the granite parapets and keeping a very low profile, is an array of eminent Trinity College academics. I have attended many public lectures given by Trinity College professors but I did not get to know about the great scientific minds until quite recently, in particular Luke O'Neill FRS, Professor of Biochemistry and Immunology. He is not only an eminent scientist on the world stage, he is a great communicator of popular science for people like me with minimal scientific knowledge. He is up there with David Attenborough and Brian Cox on television explaining the origin of life on earth and the wonders of the universe. For those unfamiliar with his work, I shall outline some of his ideas on science, the philosophy of science and what it means to be human from a purely scientific perspective.

The origin and nature of man:

Professor O'Neill's recent book, 'Humanology: A Scientist's Guide to our Amazing Existence' (2018)[11] and his subsequent public lecture on the same topic at Trinity College (2019)[12] have left all other similar books and essays on the origin of life on earth in the shade. He takes us on an amazing journey back in time when life first appeared on earth 4.2 billion years ago. I shall focus on two of his main claims. Firstly, on the origin of life on earth, he subscribes to the 'primordial soup' theory that life evolved through random chemistry. To prove his point that life on earth began as a chemical reaction, he cites the experiment carried out in 1953 by an American chemist, Stanley Miller,[13] which demonstrated that organic compounds could be synthesised from inorganic substances. That discovery seemed to imply that inorganic material could have, under ameliorating conditions, evolved into proteins, the building blocks of life. Then, evolution kicked in and cellular life took off. Around 200,000 years ago, the first humanoids appeared in Africa. Later still, the primate family split up and one species, the Neanderthals, became extinct and Homo Sapiens became the dominant species and spread across Europe some 40,000 years ago. Then, some 10,000 years, that is around 8,000 B.C., the first Mesolithic hunter-gatherers arrived in Ireland and lived in coastal settlements for three thousand years until they were displaced by waves of Neolithic migrants around 4,000 B.C.

I cannot say that Professor O'Neill is wrong in asserting that life on earth began as a chemical accident. Let me say instead that I have mental reservations about extrapolating from a test tube experiment in 1953 to the origin of life on the planet some 4.2 billion years ago. I do not believe that Miller's experiment involving a chemical reaction to radiation in a test tube recreates the beginning of life on the planet. I simply cannot comprehend how inorganic matter can, by some freak of chemistry, transmute itself into organic matter. I simply say 'Show me the data' for such a belief. I see it as an interesting hypothesis, nothing more. In research, it is axiomatic that one must not generalise from a single instance or event. It is a very big leap from a single test tube experiment in modern times to the whole of creation an estimated 4.2 billion years ago. Professor O'Neill may be an eminent scientist but he seems to be rather disingenuous in reading more into the Miller experiment than is warranted. Several scientists have questioned the validity of Miller's experiment. The data they cite is quite complex (it is on the NISL website) but it revolves around the absence of a constant electrical charge and a whole set of gases in the primitive atmosphere; they say most of the atmospheric carbon was CO_2.

My point is that scientists cannot see beyond the physical world. They do not consider metaphysical reality, philosophy, theology, sociology, or even linguistic science. They call creation a myth. For them, the biblical story about Adam and Eve is mythology. However, great minds over the centuries have not closed their minds to sacred scripture, which is accepted as divine revelation. I do not find the notion of creation at all irrational; to my mind, it seems a lot more rational than assuming that gases can, by some magical random chemical process, transform into a living organism. For Christians, the Bible is the history of God's revelation to mankind. It is special kind of history which requires biblical exegesis. The material evidence for the Bible - the evidence of the spade - is there in great profusion for anyone who visits the Middle East. In any case, religious belief does not need scientific evidence. Your either believe or you don't. We all believe many things without being absolutely able to prove them. As the celebrated scientist and theologian, Alister McGrath[14] has pointed out, you get absolute proof only in mathematics. Professor John Lennox (2019)[15] also has a lot to say on the interface of science, religion and philosophy. We all have to live with uncertainty and doubt. Science, faith and doubt are not only compatible, they hold together. As Professor O'Neill admits, religion is about 'why' we are here; science is about 'how' we are here. Moreover, it is interesting that neither Charles Darwin nor Alfred Russel Wallace ruled out Creation. Wallace speaks of 'something in the unseen universe of Spirit'. We should not forget that evolution in only a theory, not a fact.

People of faith are convinced that we all need scripture to anchor us in a world of confusing ideologies. Biblical history is not linear. It exists on several levels and it sees humans as a spiritual beings, which physicists like Richard Dawkins and Lawrence Krauss regard as crass mythology. They would want us to believe their fairy-tale, that 'everything came from nothing.' They claim that our feeble minds are unable to grasp such a profound concept and only people of superhuman intelligence, (i.e. Dawkins and Krauss) can comprehend such a notion. My response to them is: 'Rave on, one-eyed cosmologists!'

Of course, Professor O'Neill is entitled to his interpretation of human history. He is a scientist and those of us who are not into scientism see things differently. He is very much a liberal rationalist. Popular science is written for people of liberal/secularist persuasion. It is not intended for dissidents like me who look at life from a metaphysical perspective. Liberals, secularists and humanists will find 'Humanology' comforting in that it validates their rejection of God and creation. For me, the best history book is the Bible. It goes beyond the physical dimension and looks at man in the head, in the soul and in the spirit. I would remind Professor O'Neill and all those in the 'New Ireland' that believe in scientism of Hamlet's (Act.1, Sc.5) admonition to Horatio:

> There are more things in heaven and earth, Horatio
> Than are dreamt of in your philosophy (science)

Professor O'Neil also poses another very interesting question: What is the nature of man? Then with great wit and erudition, he discusses the salient traits of man based on the genes we have inherited from cave man (including Neanderthals). These he lists as follows:

Attraction and love: We are a bunch of hormones

Raising children: Metacognition needs to be nurtured

Music: It is good for social bonding and has a soothing effect on the mind

Gender: It is biological. 10% of humans are gay. Without diversity we die.

Humour: We laugh at ourselves and we make fun of our rulers and bosses.

Religion: We invented God. Faith in God is an evolved trait.

Sleeping: It washes the mind and is essential for wellbeing.

Ageing: We are all mortal; lifestyle, diet and stress control help to some extent

He concludes by stating that the human race is on the road to extinction but not in the biblical sense of the End Time. However, nobody can foretell what will happen in the future – only prophets can do that and John the Baptist was the last of the prophets. Humans may go on wrecking the planet, or we may all be wiped out by a deadly pandemic or nuclear war. Due to advances in digital technology, robots and AI, Homo Sapiens may be supplanted by Home Digitalis. We simply have no way of foretelling the future.

What I find most surprising about Professor O'Neill list is that many of the key defining attributes of humans seem to be absent, in particular the following:

Cognition, 'cogito ergo sum'; the idea that it all happens up here in the mind. We are good at creative and critical thinking, the creative imagination, problem-solving, etc. When you look into the sad eyes of an orang-utan, you get the impression that it may be wondering why it and the other apes missed on the evolutionary chain.

Conscience, free will, a natural ethical sense embedded in the human brain. We make moral choices based on an innate ethical sense below the level of consciousness that some things are inherently right or wrong. It is a natural moral sense that transcends borders and cultures. Cicero refers to it as Natural Law.

Language: There is no mention of the thing we call 'language'. Humans are unique in that they are the only 'articulate mammals'. Jean Aitchison (2008)[16] has quite a lot to say about language within an evolutionary framework, the probability of a 'language gene', and how humans are always making a hypothesis about their internalised language system.

Professor O'Neill does mention religion but he sees it as 'an evolved trait', ho, ho! He would say that, wouldn't he? He says that man invented God. However, people of faith say it is the other way round, God created the universe and all living things within it. Belief in a Supreme Being is too big a topic to discuss here. Obviously, it requires a leap of faith. However, for me, belief in creation is a more rational belief than the opposite – that everything came from nothing. My belief in creation is based not only on scripture but on copious archaeological evidence across the Middle East. The problem with scientism is that it sees only what it wants to see.

Regarding Irish people in particular, I have noticed a few traits which may be cultural or genetic. I wonder why these 'national' traits are not mentioned. They are, in no particular order the following:

- exceptional altruism and generosity. There are 10,500 registered charities in Ireland, which speaks volumes about the generosity of the Irish.
- Irish people are exceptionally creative as writers, artists, musicians, storytellers, engineers, architects, and scientists. Is creativity a Celtic gene or does it come from years of coping with hardship?
- Perhaps, even more prominent than anything else, Irish people are exceptionally patriotic. No matter how bad things are, they will always end up saying: 'Anyhow, we're the best little country in the world.' Is that national self-delusion on a grand scale or is it genuine patriotism? The history of Ireland is mostly about a fiercely independent people desperately defending their freedom, land and culture against 'dungeon, fire and sword.'

In speaking of human traits, one topic which baffles me is humanity's dark side. In Essay 3, I stated that man is the most destructive of all

God's creatures and I listed examples of the lexicon of violence. Human destructiveness covers a wide spectrum from war, genocide, ethnic cleansing, slavery, colonialism, abuse of power, murder, abortion, euthanasia, racism, exploitation, criminality, bullying, sexual assault, killing the planet and wildlife. The writer, Edgar Alan Poe describes man's destructive nature as 'perverseness'. In the short story 'The Black Cat' (1843), he argues that knowing something is wrong can be the one force that makes us do it. In the story, he tells us that he (the narrator) intentionally killed his beloved cat because he knew that he was committing a deadly sin. I have to assume that perverseness must be an innate biological process at least in a subset of humanity. In fact, I am convinced that 'perverseness' is a feature of the political leadership of the 'New Ireland'. A state that legalises human killing has to be perverse.

Finally, you may ask what all of the above has to do with living in a State that calls itself a republic. The answer goes back beyond the foundation of the Republic to the long history of the revelation of God to His chosen people and to the coming of the Messiah, Jesus of Nazareth, who mapped out the road to salvation for people and nations. The Republic of Ireland was founded on an idea - an idea embedded in sacred scripture which explains the meaning of life and what humanity must do in order to live in peace. That idea has a long history going back to the dawn of time, something that shaped our civilization and made us what we are. To understand ourselves we have to go back in time and uncover our history. Memory of the past has always been part of education and it is a key element in Christian education. However, in the 'New Ireland' the government is telling us to forget the past and the Christian tradition of Irish people which goes back to St. Patrick who came to our shores in 432 A.D. and converted our Celtic ancestors to Christianity. Now, we must not mention his name nor that of his pious disciples who in the 6th century created the a nation of 'saints and scholars'. However, the main thrust of education does not come from the State even though it can reset the curriculum along secularist lines. 'It comes from families and communities wishing to keep alive the knowledge that has made them who they are. The Constitution recognises that this is especially important in the area of religious and moral formation.'[17]

Endnotes:

1   a posteriori: The empiricist approach to the acquisition of knowledge which proceeds from known facts, based on observation, experience or experiment, for instance, Darwin's theory of evolution.

2   revolutionary epistemics: See J.T. Roberts (1977). Revolutionary epistemics and language learning. Occasional Papers 19, University of Essex.
a priori: The rationalist or non-empirical approach to the acquisition of knowledge which derives form theoretical deduction rather than from observation or experience, for instance, Chomsky's theory of an innate language acquisition device in the brain.

3   Plutarch (46-119 A.D.) was a Greek philosopher, biographer and priest at the Temple of Apollo. W. B. Yeats also paraphrases the same idea thus: 'Education is not the filling of a pail, but the lighting of a fire'.

4   In the Peoples' Republic of China, Islam is regarded as a mental illness and Muslims in the Xinjiang Province are subjected to a programme of re-education in internment camps lasting several months.

5   Eugene Duffy (2012). 'Catholic Primary Education: Facing New Challenges'. (Position papers edited by Duffy). Dublin: The Columba Press

6   Brenda O'Brien, in The Irish Times, 12.12.2020

7   Trinity College Dublin (TCD) was founded by Queen Elisabeth1 in 1592, modelled on Oxford and Cambridge. For much of its history, it was the university of the Protestant Ascendancy. It has 24 schools, offering both undergraduate and postgraduate programmes. It has a student population of 18,000. It is currently ranked by the Times Higher Education ranking criteria as the 138th best university in the world and 101st on the QS World Ranking scale.

8   University College Dublin (UCD) grew in stages out of the Catholic University of Ireland, founded in 1854 with J. H. Newman as the first rector. It became a constituent college of the National University of Ireland. It was located at Earlsfort Terrace and other inner city locations. It began moving to the new

Belfield campus in 1964 and continued to do so up to 1990. It has 34 schools and 34,00 students. It is ranked 226-250th globally by the Times Higher Education ranking criteria and 177th on the QS World University Ranking scale.

9   John Henry Newman: 'A saint for our times.' The Irish Catholic, 10.10.2019 pp.10-34.

10   QS World University Rankings 2020 for the nine universities in the Republic:
Trinity College Dublin. 101
University College Dublin 177
National University Galway 238
University College Cork 301
Dublin City University 439
University of Limerick 511-520
Maynooth University 701-750
Tech University Dublin 801-1000

11   Luke O'Neill (2018). 'Humanology; A Scientist's Guide to our Amazing Existence'. Dublin: Gill Books.

12   Luke O'Neill (2019). 'What does it mean to be human?' Public lecture in the Edmund Burke Lecture Theatre, Trinity College Dublin. Available on YouTube. Retrieved 14.12.2020

13   Stanley Miller's experiment is believed by some scientists to prove chemical evolution. He sent an electrical charge through a flask containing a chemical solution of ammonia, methane and hydrogen which induced a chemical reaction. A week later, he detected amino acids which are organic compounds that combine to form proteins and, as we know from our school days, proteins are the building blocks of life.

14   Alister McGrath (2020). 'Through a Glass Darkly: Journeys through Science, Faith & Doubt'. London: Hodder & Stoughton. The author of many books, presentations on the BBC and articles in The Times and The Telegraph, McGrath is Professor of Science and Religion at Oxford University. Like his great hero, C.S. Lewis, he comes from Belfast and his book tells how he moved from ardent Marxist to devout Christian and theologian.

15   John Lennox (2019). 'Can science explain everything?' Epsom: The Good Book Company. Professor Lennox explains how religion and science complement each other to give us a fuller understanding of the universe and the meaning of our existence.

16 Jane Aitchison (208). 'The Articulate Mammal: An Introduction to Psycholinguistics' 5th ed. Routledge.

17 Bishop Donal Murray (2012). 'The Catholic Church's Current Thinking on Educational Provision'. In Duffy et al. op. cit. p.56

130

9

ECONOMIC INEQUALITY

In the course of a Cabinet meeting on a balance of payments problem and in response to a possible solution, the former Taoiseach, Garret FitzGerald, supposedly said: 'That's fine in practice, but how will it work in theory?' Whether true or false, that remark has a lesson for all of us. We should not pay too much attention to out-of-touch theory-obsessed economists. We, the consumers, live in the real world but economists live in a world of their own devising. It is probably true that most of us have a poor grasp of economic theory but we do not have to be great at everything. We all have to adapt to the emerging green digital economy and we all have to figure out things by ourselves. With that caveat in mind, I have given myself permission to stray into the territory of economics about which I am profoundly ignorant.

A good starting point in discussing economic policy is Noam Chomsky's (2017)[1] assertion: 'The real difference between democracy and oligarchy is between poverty and wealth.' All governments, whatever their colour, owe their power to wealth. There is obviously a symbiotic relationship between economics and politics. Different schools of economics view that relationship in different ways.

Dickensian economics:

In Dicken's 'David Copperfield' (1850) we meet the redoubtable Mr. Micawber whose life principle is 'live within your means'. When annual expenditure exceeds annual income, the result is misery. Hence, the unemployed, the unemployable and all people on low income must live a life of fortitude in spite of hardship, homelessness, hungry children, squalid dwellings, extreme poverty and social inequality. Dickens paints a more vivid picture of the brutal reality of life in Victorian England in 'A Tale of Two Cities' (1859). The famous opening lies are: 'It was the best of times, it was the worst of times, it was the age of foolishness, it was the epoch of belief, it was the season of Light, it was the season of Darkness...'

In Ireland at that time, poverty was endemic and greedy landlords held the reins of power. As one historian put it, 'the situation was pregnant with wild hopes and bitter animosities.' After the Act of Union (1800), economic policy for Ireland was dictated by Westminster. In July 1845, the Whig leader, Lord John Russell became Prime Minister as the Great Famine was raging in Ireland. He appointed Charles Trevelyan to oversee the Poor Law Relief Scheme in Ireland. He was an Anglican archdeacon, who believed that the Famine was sent by the Almighty to punish the Irish for their adherence to 'popery'. His own words on this issue are: 'the judgement of God sent the calamity to teach the Irish a lesson.' He also saw the Famine as 'a mechanism for reducing surplus population.' He had a pathological dislike of the Irish and especially Roman Catholics. Apart from anti-Popery, the Prime Minister and Trevelyan believed in the free market. They argued that the Irish could not be given free food because that would destabilise market prices. Then as now, laissez-faire economics put profit before people. Lord Russell also declared that the starving Irish should become the financial burden of their own landlords and poor landlords must be protected at all costs! In February 1847, the Whig government finally realized that something had to be done and it was decided to open soup kitchens for the free distribution of soup. By July 1847, more than three million starving people were being fed every day in government soup kitchens or in soup kitchen run by the Society of Friends (Quakers).

Clearly, the economic and political affairs of a country are closely interdependent. The failure of the potato crop in Ireland caused the famine. However, natural disasters such as famine and epidemics happen. A caring government has a duty to respond appropriately in such situations but the Victorian response to the Great Famine was to ignore it, since it was 'providential'. Governments have always been very good at ignoring natural calamities. They always put the free market above the welfare to the people. Self-preservation was the name of the game in Westminster as it is in Leinster House. Politicians speak of having great empathy for the poor and the marginalised but the poor only get the crumbs that fall from the rich man's table. At least Marie-Antoinette was honest when she reportedly said of the starving peasants: 'Let them eat cake.'[2]

Keynesian economics:

Classical market-oriented economic theory held sway well into the 20th century. However, two world wars did much to promote an alternative economic model developed by John Maynard Keynes[3] who started a revolution in economic thinking in the post-war years. He took the view that the Great Depression of the 1930s was caused by a lack of investment by the government. In other words, governments should spend their way out of recession. He advocated the use of fiscal policy (i.e. government spending) in order to mitigate the adverse effects of recessions, to reduce inflation and to ensure price stability.

Events in Ireland from 1922 up to 1960 did not make the Republic a prosperous nation. The Free State struggled to convert independence into a better quality of life for its citizens. Sadly, there was no economic boom, only doom and gloom. Over 50,000 Irish people emigrated each year. Irish families faced years of austerity. It was a time of national paralysis and economic stagnation. Eamonn de Valera remained at the forefront of Irish politics from 1926 to 1959. He was an out-and-out Republican, fully in tune with the aspirations of the founding fathers of the Republic, a patriot and a man of unbending nationalist pride and conviction. However, he had little interest in economic development. His main focus was on reviving Irish nationalism, the Irish language, Irish traditional values, moral rectitude and Irish culture, down to 'dancing at the crossroads'. He often clashed with his Minister for Industry and Commerce, Seán Lemass whose predominant interest had always been economics. Lemass had furious rows with de Valera over economic policy which was protectionist and in his famous tapes (recorded in 1967), he states quite candidly that by the 1950s 'Dev was losing his grip.' It seems that de Valera did not agree that governments should spend money that they do not have. Lemass does not mention Keynes in his 'tapes' but he must have been familiar with the Keynesian doctrine of spending your way out of recession. He concedes that 'We misjudged the economic climate a great deal.' Matters came to a head in 1956 when a balance of payments crisis hit the Republic causing massive economic damage and unemployment. In 1958, with much assistance from T K Whitaker, the Department of Finance Secretary, Lemass drafted and launched the first economic development plan. Its objective was 'to secure the economic foundation of independence.' It was a totally new departure. It opened the Republic to industrial development, foreign investment, as well as boosting agricultural output, trade and tourism. Lemass went on to serve as Taoiseach from 1959 to 1966. Under his dynamic leadership, the Republic recovered its self-confidence and economic health which had languished during the de Valera years.

The Irish economy really took off when Ireland joined the European Union (the EEC, as it was known then). Membership of the EU opened the door to a massive market of 500 million consumers. Free trade and the removal of tariff barriers gave Irish exporters an enormous boost, which in turn created jobs and higher income. As EU citizens, Irish people are free to live and work in any EU member state. Irish farmers in particular benefit from direct payments under the CAP scheme. However, as the Irish economy began to match and surpass that of other less prosperous EU member states, much of the EU bounty dissipated and Ireland is now a net contributor to the EU. The Kafkaesque bureaucracy of the EU is not its only damaging trait; its promotion of liberal ideology is much more insidious. It remains to be seen whether Irish taxpayers will continue to support the autocratic EU Commission which has two main objectives: (a) protecting the Single Market and (b) diluting the nation-state. Hence, one may ask what state wishes to surrender its sovereignty to a foreign power and what state agrees to being strangled by EU regulations? These are questions that member states are already raising but the EU does not seem to be listening. A true republic must, by definition, retain national sovereignty which is perfectly possible within a European Commonwealth of member states. That is the obvious answer to the European Question, each member state retaining its national sovereignty, making its own laws and protecting its own borders. Everything else – free trade, education, travel, the right to abode, environmental policy, security, etc. can be Euro-centric. Ireland has always been part of Europe. Irish people were always European in outlook. They love European culture and they have no objection to belonging to a multi-cultural Europe. They did not become more European by joining the EU. It is time to re-set the European dream.

Sadly, we are living in an uniquely corrupt era of socio-political thinking. Authoritarianism is on the march across Europe. Democracy and human rights are in danger. Liberal governments are using misinformation and propaganda to expand executive authority and suppress dissent. Dictatorial regimes are not only in Russia, China and North Korea; they are in Europe and secularist ideology has become weapon to silence people of faith, especially Catholics, Evangelicals, Muslims and Jews. In the 'New

Ireland' there is no space for people of faith. Even in the economic domain, there is little evidence of balanced growth and shared prosperity. The Irish government seems blind to the housing crisis and the ever rising cost of living which is causing enormous distress to Irish families.

Neoliberalism:

By the 1970s, Keynesian economic theory been replaced in the USA and the UK by a drastically different economic philosophy which is called neoliberalism. It rejected the view that significant government intervention (fiscal policy) was required if employment and output targets were to be met. Neoliberalism was dedicated to free market capitalism, minimal government intervention in the economy and the privatisation of public services. It was all for free trade and globalisation. It was a revival of the classical economics of Adam Smith (1776) during the heyday of Victorian industrial and colonial expansion. Neoliberalism was like a tidal wave that came on the back of globalisation. In simple terms, neoliberalism can be defined by the slogan 'let the market prevail.' For a detailed account of its origin, history and its damaging impact on society see Chomsky (2017). 'Requiem for the American Dream.'

In Ireland, neoliberalism was viewed by those on the political left wing as rampant right-wing capitalism, something that had great appeal for politicians such as Charles Haughty, who was elected Taoiseach in 1979. He addressed the nation on national television in January 1980, saying: 'As a nation we are living away beyond our means.' That statement was quite true but it was rich coming from a man of enormous wealth accumulated, it was said, by shady deals. The 'greed is good' message of neoliberalism had a profoundly damaging impact on the Irish economy leading up to the collapse of the Celtic Tiger. I shall not dwell on the spectacular rise of the Celtic Tiger nor on its dramatic demise. Volumes have been written about that extraordinary phenomenon. To this day, most people cannot explain the Republic's fondness for a 'boom and bust' economy. The 2008 financial crisis in the Republic crisis was caused by poor economic planning, poor management and the lack of proper supervision of the economy. It was due mainly to the failure of the state to develop and diversify the domestic economy. It had always favoured as few sectors of the economy to the detriment of others. It was due to fiscal recklessness, massive borrowing, the incompetence of politicians, the greed of the bankers, speculators, property developers, business tycoons and all manner of con men, including the legal and accounting professions. It was the 'fat cats' and the IMF bailout that brought the country to its knees.

The economics of inequality:

The science of economics is no longer about the careful management of the available resources and wealth of the nation-state. The nation-state and nationalism are under constant attack by the forces of neoliberalism and globalisation. The 'New World Order' has ordained that the nation-state must submit to the gospel of neoliberalism. According to Thomas Piketty (2015)[4] right-wing (neoliberal) governments are reluctant to do anything that would interfere with the 'virtuous' mechanisms of the market. On the other hand, left wing (socialist) governments want to alleviate the misery of the poorest members of society by nationalising the means of production and taxing the rich to pay for the welfare and betterment of the least well-off. Inequality of income is not difficult to measure. An analysis of the various sources of household income shows the great divide between those at the top and the bottom of the pyramid. OECD statistics show that Ireland is as good and even better than most EU member states at generating wealth, however, the main problem is its unequal distribution.[5] The Dickensian divide between concentrated wealth and abject poverty has not ended. At present, in 2021, western governments are still telling their people the great lie: 'You've never had it so good'. Of course, that is true for those 'in the money' – the bankers, business tycoons, property developers, investment and insurance brokers, accountants, lawyers and politicians. For as long as I can remember, it seems to me that successive Irish government have become less democratic, less caring and more greedy in the pursuit of material wealth for those at the top table. Irish politicians have always been very good at looking after themselves and their friends. They seem to have an inordinate fondness for the good life, for lavish spending on junkets to far-away places, for trips to the races at Galway, Cheltenham and Ascot, for oysters and champagne, for mercs and perks. Nobody would object to rewarding them generously if they actually did something for the people they are elected to represent. However, that does not happen. The same old useless codgers are re-elected to the Dáil again and again and any new blood is generally radical left-wing zealots 'full of sound and fury signifying nothing' (Macbeth, Act 5, Sc. 5).

Irish people are still suffering from the collapse of the Celtic Tiger (2008), the IMF bailout that followed it and the austerity measures that citizens are still enduring resulting from that 'mother of all scandals'. However, Irish people are very forgiving. The same politicians are still in power. After months of political wrangling over the formation of the new government, following the General Election in May 2020, a new 'triad' government marched into Leinster House, a coalition of three political parties whose hatred of each other is slightly less than their combined hatred for all the other political parties on the opposition benches. This ménage à trois is hardly a good recipe for stable and democratic governance. Their first act in government was to award themselves a substantial pay rise. Long live the Republic!

Obviously, in the years ahead it will be very difficult for the government to keep the Irish economy on a sound footing because of the ravages of the Coronavirus pandemic and the economic fallout from Brexit. The Republic's economy was expected to grow by 6% in 2020 but the Coronavirus intervened and it grew by only 0·8%. However, much of the credit for Ireland's economic progress has been down to the success of the IDA in attracting 'foreign direct investment' in the Republic which is seen by global companies as the best country in Western Europe to invest in. All the big global players are here – Apple, Google, Facebook, PayPal, Microsoft, etc. In addition, 'Enterprise Ireland' must take the credit for the remarkable success of Irish-owned companies which it funds and supports. Irish politicians at present are very fond of referring to creating a better 'fiscal space'. However, that can be achieved by additional borrowing, raising taxes and cutting expenditure. Nobody in government is telling us that the Republic is about to experience a massive recession in 2021.

Putting aside the question as to which economic model works best in theory, (which is what many economists discuss), I see three major problems which our learned economists seem to have overlooked. The are the redistribution of wealth, the enormous national debt and the ever rising cost of living.

The Great Reset: [6]

The World Economic Forum decided in June 2020 that now is the time for a 'great reset' of capitalism. The basic idea is to reform the faltering global economy by moving towards a 'stakeholder capitalism' which looks beyond the traditional focus on maximising profit for shareholders. It promises a utopian state in which 'you will own nothing, and you will be happy.' It aims to do the following: (a) establish and coordinate global free trade, (b) ensure that investments advance equality and sustainability. This means building a green economy and (c) harness innovation to address health and social issues. It is not difficult to see how the proposed 'great reset' would be a terrifying prospect for the nation state. A coalition of big business and big tech obviously seeks to enslave the entire population. The 'Great Reset' which has been designed by a global élite to subdue all of humanity which it does by coercive measures regarding the market, trade, wealth creation, etc. all of which drastically limit individual freedom and the welfare of the common people. It is an attempt to impose socialism and dismantle the traditional nation-state. Its godfathers meet annually at the 'World Economic Forum' which seeks to justify the economic dictatorship that is overseen by the 'International Monetary Fund'. Obviously the redistribution of wealth is not on the radar of the IMF which will allow governments to borrow any amount of money in order to mortgage to entire country to it and thus make future generations keep on paying off the national debt. The crassness of the 'great reset' has been described by Archbishop Carlo Viganò [7] as follows: 'This Great Reset, desired by the globalist elite, represents the 'final revolution' with which to create a shapeless and anonymous mass of slaves connected to the internet, confined to the house, threatened by an endless series of pandemics designed by those who have the miraculous vaccine ready…Lies, deception, violence, death: this is the harsh reality of evil before which people of good will can only be horrified.'

Irish economic problems:

The Irish economy is dominated by a small group of very wealthy people and by large global corporations. They get substantial tax breaks and some pay very little tax. The concept of an 'even playing field' does not apply. International companies operating in Ireland can claim that the parent company is located in the Cayman Islands or some other offshore destination and that company tax is levied and paid there. The Republic has been named a 'tax haven' in a variety of reports. Small Irish businesses and small farmers do not get any tax breaks and are often forced to sell their produce at below the cost of production.

The problem of national indebtedness does not seem to bother our government at all. It will go on borrowing as if there was no tomorrow. Sadly, there is a tomorrow and it is not going to be much fun for Irish taxpayers now or in the future. Economically, the Republic is living on borrowed time, with a spiralling national debt of €239 billion, before factoring in the additional cost to the exchequer of the Coronavirus pandemic and Brexit. The Republic has the highest debt per capita of any country in the euro zone at €48,000 per head.

What worries ordinary people most and governments least is the spiralling cost of living. The Republic is a very expensive country to live in. Goods and services cost at least 25% more than the EU average. Home ownership has always been an objective of Irish people however it is now beyond the reach of people on average or low income. The cost of housing is astronomical and rents in cities and towns can start at €1,000 and run as high as €2,000 a month. Over the past ten years, wages in the public sector have increased by a mere 4·5%. An average family (two parents and two children) living in Dublin will spend at least €1, 800 on food and bills. Now, let us suppose you are a mid-career Primary School teacher in Dublin and your gross annual salary in €36,000. After deduction of income tax, PRSI and USC and allowing a tax credit of €275 your net annual income is €18,404 (€1533 per month). An expert mortgage broker has advised me that a modest semi-detached house in the outer suburbs of Dublin will cost in the region of €400,000. The monthly mortgage repayment on such a property is €1,500 over 30 years. In order to survive that family would need a monthly income of €3,300 (€1,500 for mortgage and €1.800 cost of living). The problem for most earners is that the government has imposed a mortgage lending rule that you can only borrow 3·5 times your gross annual salary so that you would need to have a job paying €100.000 p.a. in order to qualify for the mortgage. Not many jobs in the city are paying even close to that amount. The so-called 'Generation Rent' is stuck on a treadmill of working hard but unable to achieve the aspiration of home ownership

Since the government takes back almost half of your total income, you rightly feel entitled to a roof over your head, sufficient cash for basic food, clothing, free medical and dental care, free schooling, subsidised transport and possibly an affordable one-week family holiday in West Cork or Connemara. Of course, nothing is free in Ireland unless you are bottom of the pile on Social Welfare, receiving c. €800 per month plus a rent allowance. When you add up the cost of house insurance, medical insurance, property tax, utilities, and keeping an old Toyota on the road, you will need a monthly income of around €3,300 but your net monthly income is only half of that amount! Unless you win the lotto, your only option to forget about purchasing a house and either move in with your parents and live in the spare room, or else head for greener fields in the Gulf, or Australia or possibly Brunei, where income tax is unknown and where everything, including housing, is free.

Today, in the Republic, most people are finding it difficult to survive in an country where the main focus is on making enough money in order to stay out of debt rather than living well. It does not have to be like that. I have seen how primitive people in Borneo with no money live well in their ancestral homeland, the rainforest. They live off the bounty of the rainforest and they trade game, fish, handicrafts etc. for the few things they need to buy, such as salt. Of course, they live happily without television or the internet. They grow their own food, make their own bread and beer and use their own home-made herbal medicines and soap. Their normally have large families and live in long houses, where everything is shared. They are poor but healthy and cancer is virtually non-existent. Their children receive a good education in Mission Schools run by Catholic and Protestant churches. My point it that we need to reset the Irish economy on our terms rather than on IMF and EU terms. Life is not about making money, it is about living well and making the most of the nation's natural resources. For me, the only real economy is one based on a harmonious relationship with nature, getting back to the Edmund Burke idea of the 'little platoons'- local communities working together on cooperative enterprises.

We do not have to live in a Republic that has become a money-grabbing monster that sucks the lifeblood of ordinary people by excessive taxation, VAT on everything you buy, a vile property tax, mortgage madness, Vulture funds and a government spending vast amounts on vanity projects, for instance the new National Children's Hospital in Dublin.[8] What a fiasco! It has become 'the mother of all scandals'. Initially the cost of building the new hospital was stated to be €650 million but now, four years later, it is projected to be €2·4 billion. The man responsible, the Minister of Health, Simon Harris keeps on repeating that the overspend is due to 'hyperinflation' in construction costs! Only a fool would sign off on a contract without first ascertaining and agreeing on the total cost of the project and its date of completion. Of course, Mr. Harris was out of his dept in the Department of Health, which under his direction became utterly shambolic, just like a Third World institution. He was running around like a headless chicken promoting his abortion scheme instead of looking after his Department. If you were ill, the last place you wanted to be was on trolley waiting in a public hospital corridor for 20 hours or more to be seen by a junior house doctor. I do not know how Irish taxpayers can trust a Minister and a government that shows such wanton disregard for public money. Where did the money go? Did it go into deep pockets? In any other modern democracy, the Minister responsible would have been fired for gross incompetence. Of course, that does not happen in the 'New Ireland'. The old boy network looks after its own.

Clearly, the decision to build the new children's hospital on the St. James's Hospital campus was an unmitigated disaster. It seems to have been designed as a vanity project to show that Ireland has the most expensive hospital in the world. The government obviously did not think very much about the needs of children requiring medical attention. It did not consider the world and the psychology of the child. No child wants to be holed up in a seven-storey high tower block in the most congested and polluted area of the city. The area has a certain Victorian ambiance but the new concrete hospital stands in stark contrast to the existing St. James's buildings and the surrounding Victorian artisan dwellings. Everyone is baffled as to why the government insisted on building the new hospital in the wrong place when it could have been built at a fraction of the cost on a greenfield site off the M50. Anyone with half a brain knows very well that children need to be near nature. Recent research in Sweden and Germany shows that there is a strong correlation between the wellness of children and their closeness to nature, to trees, to woodland, to green fields, hills, birds, and animals, etc. A sick child benefits from fresh air and some exposure to the sights and sounds of mother nature. The whole project was a massive mistake – wrong location, wrong design, wrong costing, but would they listen? Of course, not. The hospital, which may or may not open in 2023, will be a monument to the arrogance, stubbornness and ineptitude of the government and the Board charged with its oversight.

All the blame cannot be attributed to Mr. Harris. The Cabinet under the then Taoiseach, Leo Varadkar, approved the deal. He and his cabinet not only chose to allow the cost of the Children's Hospital to escalate exponentially but also failed spectacularly to deal the two most pressing problems in the Republic - housing crisis and the hospital / national health crisis. How can they sleep at night knowing that 10,000 Irish people are homeless? They have obviously closed their eyes to the homeless people sleeping in doorways or in shelters provided by charities. They have shown little concerns for the poor tenants in rent arrears waiting for the sheriff to call with an eviction order. The have not grasped the disillusion and despair of ordinary people who can no longer afford to pay their monthly mortgage, the property tax and the ever increasing cost of living. They have been and still are blind to the fact that almost half of the population is in debt and struggling to make ends meet. There are none so blind as those who do not wish to see. Every social worker can tell you that there are pockets of poverty in every Irish city and town that are almost as dire as those in sub-Saharan Africa. But the great and the good in Leinster

House have chosen to ignore the appalling economic inequality and simply ensured that their devout followers, the well-to-do class, get their slice of the salami. Now, things are even worse as a new carbon tax demanded by the Green Party will drive many families over the edge. Are Irish taxpayers getting value for money, or are they giving the government licence to squander billions of euro on vanity projects? That is a question every voter should ponder.

I could go on about many other vanity projects that the government is undertaking, for instance of act of barbarism in destroying urban villages in Dublin in order to create more space for buses and cars, thereby creating more traffic congestion and more pollution. The people are up in arms and have said NO again and again. They have insisted that our suburban villages are not bus corridors; they are communities but the 'little pharaohs' in the NTA will not listen. They say that residents have been consulted but that is not true. I live in one of the designated areas and nobody has consulted me at all. Our local TDs promised to fight the project 'tooth and nail' but somebody at the top table has insisted that the act of urban vandalism must proceed as planned. All the ancient trees along the route, all the Victorian lampposts, boundary walls and potions of front garden will be demolished. In the 'New Ireland' buses and cars come before people. Modern cities like Stockholm and Singapore have shown how traffic access to the to the city centre can be restricted and properly regulated. Do we want a concrete jungle or a city which preserves its historic buildings and streetscapes, the city the James Joyce fondly described, the city with a rich architectural legacy that foreign visitors rave about.

Endnotes:

1   Noam Chomsky (2017: 11). 'Requiem for the American Dream: The 10 Principles of the Concentration of Wealth & Power. New York: Seven Stories Press.

2   Marie-Antoinette may have been referring to 'gur cake' - a cheap and popular confection. Terence P. Dolan (2006:116) suggests that the Dublin word 'gurrier' may be derived from 'gur cake' which was commonly associated with children from deprived families in Dublin.

3   John Maynard Keynes (1936). 'The General Theory of Employment, Interest and Money'. University of Chicago Press.

4   Thomas Piketty (2015). 'The Economics of Inequality'. Cambridge, MAS: The Belknap Press of Harvard University Press.

5   The OECD data for 2020 shows the ratio of the average income of the richest 10% to the poorest 10%. It shows Norway (6.1) is the most equal country in the world, South Africa (33.1) is the most unequal, and Ireland (9.4) is in line with most EU countries.

6   The 'Great Reset' of capitalism is a proposed global plan for redrawing the economic map of the world, based on the ideas of Professor Klaus Schwab and the World Economic Forum.

7   Carlo Viganò, Rome, 25th November, 2020. Translated and reported by Dr. Robert Moynihan, Letter 41, The Moynihan Letters, 2nd December, 2020. MoynihanReport@gmail.com

8   St. James's Hospital, in the old Dublin Liberties, was originally a poorhouse before becoming a foundling hospital in 1727. He original building was enlarged in 1803 and in 1827 it was taken over as a poorhouse by the South Dublin Union and was much used by the starving population during the Great Famine. It was occupied by the Irish Volunteers during the Easter Rising 1916. It was extensively remodelled in 1953 and in the mid-eighties several smaller hospital in Dublin closed and were relocated to St. James's.

9   Eilish O'Regan in the Irish Independent, 14.11.2020. p.10

10

UNANSWERED QUESTIONS

What is interesting about modern 'liberal' discourse is not what is being talked about but what is NOT being talked about. We hear and read a lot about 'moving on' in the 'New Ireland'. We hear a lot about liberalism, secularism, modernism and rationalism. We hear and read a lot about pluralism, equality and political correctness. We hear and read a lot about the government's 'progressive' policies and planning. However, nobody is talking about the erosion the nation state, the erosion of native culture and Christian principles, the legalisation of human killing and the decriminalisation of blasphemy. It is assumed that all of these topics are now an integral part of the 'New Ireland' mindset and must not be raised in parliament, or in the media or even in polite conversation.

Being an alien in the 'New Ireland', I have a lot of unanswered questions. However, I shall not raise any of the ultimate questions about the meaning of life, the nature of being, the universe beyond our planet, etc. I shall leave all those unanswered questions to philosophers, theologians and scientists. My 'disruptive' questions relate mostly to the here and now, why things happen - the sort of questions that an alien might ask on arriving by accident in the Republic of Ireland. The question that baffle me are the following:

- Why do Irish people allow the State to be ruled by a 'ship of fools'? – Plato's words, not mine.

- Why did Ireland surrender national sovereignty to a foreign power in Brussels?
- The 'Irish Question' remains unanswered. Are Irish people content to accept a two-state Ireland?
- Why would the God-fearing people of Northern Ireland ever want to join a dysfunctional secularist State south of the border?
- Why do Irish people prefer modern liberal/secularist ideology to traditional Christian democratic ideology?
- Why do Irish people remain silent when the ruling elite tears up many of the fundamental human rights enshrined in the Constitution?
- Who do Irish people allow the government to legalise and normalise criminal activities, in particular human killing (i.e. abortion, infanticide and euthanasia), blasphemy and sexual practices against the order of nature?
- Why do Irish people not insist on representative democracy?
- Why do Irish people need an upper chamber of government - a body of senile men and women not nominated by the people but by the Taoiseach and various privileged bodies?
- Why do Irish people allow an unelected body called a Citizens' Assembly, which has no authority nor competence whatever, to dictate government policy on socio-political matters? And, even more obscene, why does nobody object to having the recommendations of that unelected body ratified by a biased joint Oireachtas Committee?
- Why do Irish people allow the ruling elite to govern by referenda which are rigged by wording designed to deceive and by unrelenting government propaganda and lies?
- Why does the Attorney General endorse whatever legal precedents the government establishes by a flawed process?

- Why does the government spend most of its time and energy on propagating its secularist ideology rather than doing what governments are supposed to do – looking after the welfare of the people, especially by focussing on the housing crisis, the health and hospital crisis, the mental health crisis, the upsurge in crime and lawlessness and the abandonment of rural Ireland?

- Why has the government created a two-tier state, where the rich get richer and the poor get poorer by a commitment to neoliberalism?

- Why is the only test of good government seen as wealth creation? Have we forgotten the lines from Oliver Goldsmith's poem 'The Deserted Village' (1770):

> Ill fares the land to hastening ills a prey
> Where wealth accumulates and men decay.

- Why are modern 'liberals' so illiberal and so intolerant?

My thesis in this collection of essays is that Irish democracy is fundamentally broken. It is no longer representative democracy. It is top-down authoritarianism which has managed to engineer public consent by effective propaganda and brainwashing. The government has all the big guns on its side, not only unlimited financial backing but the approval of the Attorney General. The ruling coalition is propped up by a battery of highly paid but unelected advisers, communications consultants and RP gurus, all singing from the same hymn sheet. I am saying that the Republic of Ireland today is in chaos politically, socially and morally.

A true republic is marked by a love of family and mankind. We should feel a sense of loss at every death. Human killing is anathema to a true republic but the Republic of Ireland has legalised human killing. Furthermore, it has systematically removed some of the fundamental rights enshrined in Articles 41, 42, and 44 of the Irish Constitution and it is adding new 'liberal' laws to the statute books. Any mention of God is avoided like the plague even though the founding fathers in 1916 placed the republic under the patronage of the Most High God. Now, in 2021, it is very convenient to blame God, the Bible, the Church and people of faith for all the social ills that liberalism has created in the 'New Ireland'. Some feature writers in the secular press delight in distorting the moral teaching of the church. For instance, in the Irish edition of The Times, Lise Hand[1] claimed that the pro-life movement was a Popish plot to control and suppress women's reproductive rights and choices. But, of course, Ms. Hand is speaking on behalf of the fake feminists whose views are regularly reported in the print media and on RTE chat shows. The church has never condoned violence against women. Fake feminists obviously regard the deliberate killing of unborn human life as a woman's choice.

By now you will have realised that I have a problem with modern liberalism - a belief system that incorporates secularism, scientism and humanism. I see it as a deadly virus that dulls the mind and prevents rational thinking. It is the very opposite of classical liberalism which no longer exists. The keyword that is missing in the lexicon of modern liberalism is RESPECT. The fundamental tenet of classical liberalism was RESPECT. It held that human beings must always respect those who differ from them in race, religion, language, world view and culture. In Ireland, that meant that we should always follow the ancient Irish tradition which is summed up in the phrase 'live, and let live.' In a real republic, nobody gets killed. Nobody is discriminated against because of gender, the colour of their skin, or their native language, or their belief system or their traditions and customs. Our teachers told us about civility and good manners. We were told to speak the truth and mind our language. Sometimes our teachers went too far and put manners on us with the cane or strap. I am told that the Christian Brothers were good at that sort of thing. Sadly, the old notions of respect, decency and truth have gone out the window in the 'New Ireland'. We now have new norms which do not require us to behave in a civilised manner but encourage us to mock God, to make fun of religion, to call people of faith 'irrational' and to be guided by a liberal/secularist media which says it is 'normal' to blaspheme, to kill unwanted foetal life, to legalise the 'mercy killing' of frail older people and people with significant disability. I am glad that I am an alien. For me, such abominations are indicative of a headlong race to the bottom. We are no longer a true republic which adheres to the fundamental attributes of national and popular sovereignty as set out by the founding fathers of the Republic at Easter 1916.

My most worrying question is: Where are we heading? Are we going to leave our destiny in the hands of a ruling elite that is transforming what was once a democratic republic based on Christian principles and values into a godless secularist state? One hears a good deal these days about 'stepping up' and 'moving on' in the so-called 'New Ireland'. One hears a good deal about 'pluralism' and 'a progressive state', freedom 'to choose', and 'political correctness'. Of course, these terms belong to the lexicon of liberal/secularist ideology. They are as fake as the 'liberal' people who invented them. I wonder whether Irish people themselves want to 'move on'; to reject all their traditional values and moral constraints and embrace the liberal/secularist ideology of the ruling elite. However, that cannot be the case since at least 80% of Irish citizens profess to be people of faith. They believe in the Law of God, namely, the Ten Commandments. They know that human killing, blasphemy, same-sex marriage, discrimination, falsehood and the indoctrination of school children are an abomination in any society, yet they have given the ruling elite the power to legalise all of those subhuman practices.

The end of an era:

When I look around at the emerging 'New Ireland', it seems to me that the ruling elite has created a two-tier society, in which, in theory, all people are equal but in practise some are more equal than others. The 'New Ireland' is a nation of 'insiders' and 'outsiders'. I have said that the 'New Ireland' is a cold place for people of faith. They are living in a cultural wilderness, cut off from their traditional Christian values, wisdom and enlightenment. The Republic today is in steady irreversible decline, stagnation and decay. It has lost its soul, its moral compass, its common decency and its respect for life. The old 'virtues' of truth, integrity, tolerance, modesty, respect and restraint are no more. Everything that was beautiful and uplifting has been torn down and destroyed. Many people are leading empty, aimless lives, chasing success, fame, money and pleasure. They are dictated to by liars, false prophets, liberal politicians, fake feminists and 'little pharaohs'. The Republic is now a country of contradictions. It preaches equality and humanity but it practises human killing. It preaches democracy but it prescribes correct 'secularist' behaviour. It aspires to national unity but surrenders sovereignty to a foreign power. What can one say about a state which has declared that unwanted unborn babies are less human than the rest of us and must be terminated? A state that legalises human killing (abortion, infanticide and euthanasia) is barbaric and evil.

The new normal:

In the past, our universities were 'seats of learning'. Their goal was the cultivation of wisdom but now their main goal is professional training and wealth creation. They are colleges of careers and not real universities. University students today are noted for bad manners, foul language and binge drinking. Our university ranking, which in former time was among highest in the world, has reached Third World levels. We have 'moved on' it seems to regard ignorance and arrogance as desirable human attributes. I have described the current Oireachtas as an elite assembly which rules by stealth, arrogance, falsity and self-interest. It puts prejudice before principle; it puts the propagation of its secularist ideology before the welfare of the people. That assertion on my part seems harsh but I am not alone in making it. For instance, the editor of the Irish Independent refers to Leo Varadkar's Fine Gael party as 'pickled by power, arrogance and grubbiness.'[2]

It is never easy to change a grubby political system and a destructive ideology the feeds on populism. What are normal people supposed to do? I am not recommending the storming of parliament nor the public hanging of the ruling elite from the splendid Victorian lampposts on Merrion Square. What I am recommending is something a lot more nuanced. I am recommending an approach not based on liberal/secularist ideology but rather on the fundamental human belief, below the level of consciousness, that some things are inherently right or wrong. I am speaking of a natural moral sense that transcends borders and cultures. The idea of innate moral responsibility goes back to Cicero who refers to it as 'Natural Law'. We know to our cost that it is always unwise to go against nature. However, the history of mankind is a long tale of brute force. History shows us that man is the most destructive of all God's creature. In Essay 3, I mentioned the lexicon of violence, crime, mayhem and murder that exists in every language. Homo Sapiens has not always acted rationally.

In my essays I talk about the shambolic national health service, the housing crisis, the scandal of forcing families to live in 'emergency accommodation', the abandonment of rural Ireland and the phasing out of disability and mental healthcare services and funding. I speak of the two-tier state in which the rich get richer and the poor get poorer. All of these manifestations are a shocking indictment of a government that has abandoned all pretence of being caring and even-handed. It is my contention that the 'New Ireland' is a sham republic noted for endemic ineptitude and corruption. When a government minister or a Supreme Court judge is caught breaking the law, they are not punished.[3] Their offence is written off as an 'error of judgment'. However, if a poor women is caught taking an unpaid item from a shop or supermarket to feed her hungry children she is sent to prison.

Now we have a Constitutional crisis. The Republic no longer protects the right to life of all Irish people, born and unborn. The Constitution no longer protects the norms of democracy but legalises human killing, blasphemy and same-sex marriage. The 'liberal' government regards civility, truth and equality of esteem for all as outdated notions. With the full backing of deluded scientists, disgruntled feminists, the gay lobby and a media steeped in fake news it is determined to transform the Republic into a servile secularist state. It is committed to the killing not only of the unborn but to the killing of God, the killing of religion and the killing of moral formation in schools. It is no longer government by the consent of the governed. It is government by 'little pharaohs.' If they actually did something for the betterment of society, one might ignore their empty rhetoric. However, they do nothing. It is charities that are preventing the state from toppling over the edge. The 'little pharaohs' on the left are even more doctrinaire and dogmatic than those in the ruling coalition and they promote even more pernicious socio-political policies. However, they actually do nothing to solve the problems that bedevil the state. Their only contribution is grandstanding. Most of the TDs sit on their fat backsides in the Dáil and enjoy the good life that working class voters have bestowed on them. The neo-Marxist socialists on the left are even more self-serving than the crony neoliberal capitalists on the right. Between them stands Sinn Féin, the so-called Republican party. At first, that party seemed to be on the right track and people were looking to it as an alternative to the two political parties that have ruled the Republic since Independence; both of which were equally mired in 'gombeenism'[4]. However, Sinn Féin has lost the plot. It is no longer a democratic political party. Its politburo expels members who dissent from its policies. It has renounced ties with the IRA but it lacks moral credibility and its leadership was foremost in the mad rush to legalise abortion in the Republic.

Taking back control:

The most difficult question of all is what can be done to take back the country from the secularist elite. It will not be easy to dislodge an establishment that thrives on falsity and endemic corruption, a government that is committed to normalising the abnormal, a government that excels at lying and defending the indefensible. It is hard to see a way forward on the political front unless some of the small emerging political parties manage to win popular support. The common people are trapped in a spider's web of deceit, misinformation and misrule coming at them from the government and from its 94 statutory bodies which operate on behalf of the government under the relevant minister in central government. I have said that a fish rots from the head down. The tentacles of government reach to every corner society and the body politic has no say whatever in the manner in which statutory bodies work. For instance, the HSE is obliged to provide an abortion service simply because it is government policy. The problem is not the HSE, it is the government.

As a writer, all I can do is to suggest a possible way forward. The following ideas, therefore, are simply 'possibly useful suggestions.' Fundamental to my thinking on rebuilding a true republic are the following:

1. Cicero's concept of Natural Law. The rule of law is essential for civilised living. Without law-abiding citizens, a state descends into chaos. However, the rule of law becomes void if it is subordinated to a particular ideology. Therefore, it is essential that fundamental human rights are protected in a charter that we call the Constitution. Fundamental Constitutional laws cannot be extinguished since they are innate, part of the blueprint in the human brain. Every human being knows intuitively that some things are inherently right or wrong, in other words, human beings possess a natural moral sense that transcends all races, borders and cultures. Natural Law is innate, not man-made. It is part of human

inheritance; it is what makes us human. All jurisprudence is, or should be, based on Natural Law.

2. A focus on truth. One of the most fundamental principles of a true republic is the upholding of truth. Good governance must be based on truth and not on falsity, fake news, distortion and euphemism. It is my contention that Irish people today are living in a sham republic. Falsity, like a deadly virus, is in the air we breathe. New norms are created by simply changing the meaning of words so that black means white and common words such as 'liberal', 'marriage', 'equality', 'progressive; etc mean the exact opposite of their definition in the Oxford English Dictionary. The most abused word in the cultural lexicon of liberalism is 'progressive' which sees social reform as the legalising of abortion, same-sex marriage, euthanasia, the secularisation of the school curriculum and the systematic indoctrination of pupils. The government's most favoured form of lying is euphemism, for instance, referring to the deliberate killing of the unborn as the 'termination of pregnancy'. The Abortion Act (2018) does not kill an abstract notion called 'pregnancy'; it kills a real human being.

3. Representative democracy: Real democracy is bottom up, not top down. Hence, it is necessary to devolve power from the Oireachtas to the people, to the 'little platoons' which Edmund Burke speaks of. Sadly, the Oireachtas has always had its fair share of 'little pharaohs' especially in the Department of Health and the Department of Education. It is time to reframe the dynamic of the relationship between the central government (the ruling elite) and the people (the local community). Imposing decisions from the centre (the Oireachtas) without any support from the people is a form of authoritarianism. The practice of using an unelected body called a 'Citizens' Assembly' to shape public opinion is a cynical abuse of power by the government as is the practice of packing

Oireachtas Committees with members selected by the government to do its bidding. As for the Senate, who wants to listen to the ranting of senile and puffed-up grandees who do not speak for the people but for their special interest? That undemocratic Senate should be abolished or radically reformed.

4. Moral responsibility: The Irish Republic is a secular state based on moral principles which are encoded in the Bible as the Ten Commandments. The Bible is believed by people of faith to be the word of God and 80% of Irish people profess to be people of faith; in other words, they believe in metaphysical reality. It is normal and natural for a Constitution to respect the religious beliefs and practices of the majority of its citizens while at the same time not impinging on the belief system of 'unbelievers.' Hence, a true republic should respect the principles of religious freedom and freedom of conscience as set out in the 1937 Constitution, which places the Republic under the patronage of the Most High God.

5. National unity: A basic principle of a true republic is national sovereignty. No nation can allow any part of its territory to the ruled or occupied by a foreign power. However, the Free State in 1921 agreed to partition the island of Ireland into two separate states. Of course, one understands why that solution to the 'Irish Question' was viewed as the only way to bring closure to the War of Independence. However, we know that the British were never good at borders. The border between the six northern counties and the south was seen at the time as a temporary arrangement. However, we now know that there is nothing more permanent than a 'temporary arrangement.' Partition has been bad for all Irish people. It is economically insane and until the Good Friday Agreement, Northern Ireland was politically an apartheid state. At the same time, it is hard to see how upright Protestants in the north should ever want to be part of a secularist state in the south.

Joining the European Union has been good for Ireland economically but politically it has been a betrayal of national sovereignty. Having endured 'dungeon, fire, and sword' under foreign occupation for 400 years, it seem baffling that Ireland should have willingly surrendered national sovereignty to a foreign power in Brussels in 1973. Irish people were always part of Europe and were always European in outlook. But the European Union is a dictatorship which imposes its sclerotic rules on all member states, from the size an apple to the amount of lead in a pencil. The Irish government uses its membership of the EU to justify its fiscal policy, its property tax, its legalisation of abortion etc. We must be good Europeans and we must not object to EU harmonisation. Consequently, if the Finns eat raw cod for breakfast, we must do likewise! I shall not go on about the absurdity of the EU monster; it was laid bare in the Brexit debate. However, if the EU ever becomes a federation of independent European states which allows its members to make their own laws, protect their own borders and engage in free trade and cooperative ventures and programmes such as the Erasmus Programme, I would view all of that as positive and progressive.

6. For me the most fundamental human right is the right to life which is the cornerstone of every Constitution. If the right to life is removed from the Constitution, all other rights become meaningless since if you are not allowed to live, you forfeit all other human rights. Have we forgotten all the depredations of the Holocaust?[5] I have been to Auschwitz and I have seen what a perverted ideology can do. The mass-killing of the unborn is proof that the Republic of Ireland is no longer a true republic; it is a dictatorship masquerading as a republic.

7. Finally, I believe that it is futile trying to persuade 'liberal' politicians to respect the Christian traditions and culture of Irish

people. They are quite incapable of engaging in rational argument and they have lost all moral compass. They actually believe their own lies. The best strategy is to ignore them and focus instead on the restoring the faith of ordinary people at local level. In a true republic, power flows from the people, from the grassroots. Ordinary people must never forget that they are not powerless. They should learn from Václav Havel's Greengrocer[6] how to 'live in truth' while the state dances its merry way to self-destruction. In order to survive, people may have to live 'within a lie' i.e. within a corrupt system but at the same time they must keep within themselves the power to remedy their own powerlessness. Power is effective only insofar as citizens are willing to submit to it. Part of every human being yearns for freedom, truth and self-dignity. Official power is eroded when those in the ruling elite begin to notice and fear the power of the powerless.

The concept of power, truth and self-belief begins in the family and extends to the parish – 'the family of families'. In Essay 2 and 6, I have referred to Edmund Burke's (1790) view that the best life begins in the 'little platoons' by which he means the family, church, the parish and the local community. From the grassroots, democracy percolates upwards to the local county council and to the electoral constituency and eventually to the central government. If that system worked, political parties could no longer impose their chosen candidates on the electorate. The 'little platoons' is a good metaphor for ordinary people at local level deciding what is best for the community, working together in a close unit that gets things done, in a spirit of co-operative concern, fellowship and self-belief. We have seen how leaders like Daniel O'Connell and Charles Stewart Parnell were able to break the stranglehold of the ruling elite by unseating the oppressive members of parliament and replacing them with honest members from the community and not from the landlord class as in the past. That approach, in my view, is the best strategy to take back the country from the liberal/secularist elite and in the process reinvent a true republic.

What I see is a grim picture of a republic rushing headlong to its eventual destruction. I see a deeply divided state at war with itself. My requiem is for a true republic that no longer exists; it fact, it never existed. It was a dream by the leaders of the Easter Rising 1916. My requiem is for the men and women who fought for Irish freedom in 1916 and in 1919-21 - the patriots who died a hundred years ago and whose dream of a true republic died with them.

Irish eyes are no longer smiling. Everywhere I go, I see sad faces, bewilderment and resignation. I hear the silence of the broken spirit, the broken reed. I also hear the deafening silence of the Catholic hierarchy, the Protestant churches and the National Bible Society on the government's plan to transform a Christian nation into a secularist state. Democracy is a delicate plant that withers when power is concentrated in the hands of a ruling elite which spends all its time propagating its particular ideology. On all sides, I seen a nation in free fall culturally, morally and economically. On all sides, I see the deconstruction of Christian Ireland. I see the symptoms of a society that has lost all moral compass, a sick society obsessed with normalising such horrendous practices as human killing, blasphemy and same-sex marriage. However, the wheels of justice grind slowly.[7] I know from history what happens when a ruling elite legalises evil practices. I know that evil always destroys itself in the end. It will probably take some time, perhaps years, for normal people to wake up to the cancer that is liberalism / secularism. It took the USA 400 years to abolish slavery. I hope it does not take the Irish state that long to restore a true republic. The country is currently in a very bad place. It needs spiritual healing. It needs to move from darkness to light – to the light of Christ (Lumen Christi).

In my essays, I am not saying anything new about modern liberalism that has not already been more fully articulated by such eminent scholars as Jordan Peterson in Canada and John Waters in Ireland or about neoliberalism by Noam Chomsky in the USA and Thomas Piketty in France. My objective is simply to spell out in plain English the pernicious influence that modern liberalism/secularism is having on Irish society. I have three main objections to modern liberalism:

(a) I abhor its 'liberal' pretensions, fake news, counter culture and political correctness.

(b) I object to its deliberate undermining of traditional social values rooted in religion, spiritual values and metaphysical reality, and most of all

(c) I reject its endorsement of human killing by abortion, infanticide and euthanasia.

All so-called 'liberals' today, whether on the right-wing or left-wing, are equally doctrinaire and illiberal. Modern liberalism/secularism is a global destructive ideology. It has created world chaos by legalising human killing, violence, environmental destruction and cultural indoctrination. It is utterly perverse. It promotes a culture of outrage, offence, intellectual dishonesty and moral depravity. It operates by stealth, fake news, counter-culture and it establishes 'new norms' based on political correctness.

I am still unsure as to what to say about the final question in my list above: Why are modern 'liberals' so illiberal, so intolerant, so assertive, so angry and so abusive? I could say that they are vain men and women who seek solace in vice, alcohol, drugs and self-delusion. However, that would be grossly unfair and untrue. It is not in my nature to denigrate other human beings. I have noticed, however, that the more aggressive modern 'liberals' are forever seeking validation, conformity and affirmation. I think the answer may be found in an understanding of the modern psyche. In this context, two related ideas spring to mind, (a) narcissism and (b) the Jungian idea of the subconscious. Narcissism is a craving for admiration, self-importance, power and prestige. It is marked by a superiority complex, extreme selfishness, self-delusion, an inflated ego and a lack of empathy. Carl Yung takes all of the above a step deeper. He speaks of the 'shadow' – the undiscovered self. In his psychology, the 'shadow' is the unknown dark side of one's personality. It is a destructive force that is dark, irrational, anti-social, wild and lawless. It is 'the beast within'. It is fed by repressed collective values which it projects onto others. It is the hidden deepest darkest self which remains lurking under one's external personality. Of course, Jung's 'shadow' fits perfectly with Christian teaching. We are all prone to evil and sinfulness but people of faith can control their dark thoughts and desires by the grace of God. The problem with atheists, humanists and secularists is that they have no means of controlling or mitigating their malign psychological projections. They cannot stand the fact that people of faith are at peace with their Maker, with themselves and with the world. People of faith are not 'woo woo' spiritualists. They are guided by the testimony God which is revealed in the Bible. They do not listen to false prophets or one-eyed cyclopes which I have referred to a few times in my essays. I thought at first that I was being overly provocative in comparing modern liberals to myopic cyclopes, but I was happy to discover that the famous writer, Karl Ove Knausgaard, has recently published an interesting essay on the same subject in a collection of essays entitled 'In the Land of the Cyclops'.[8] The author is Norwegian but has been living in Sweden which he describes as a nation of 'hatred and fear' under the thumb of myopic philistines. He satirises the intolerance and self-righteousness of Swedish liberals along with their modern psyche, their narcissism, their vacuous cancel-culture and their black-and-white thinking. He says: 'The cyclopes get angry and hurl rocks at those who say something they don't like or don't understand.' The same thing happen not only in Sweden but also in the USA, the UK and Ireland. The screaming banshees will be out in force, brandishing sharpened billhooks to cut down aliens like me and Knausgaard and John Waters, who object to having to live in world full of monsters.

I know that I am a voice in the wilderness, a disruptive voice that our liberal government and media will do their utmost to silence. The government is in charge of the narrative and the media echoes its secularist ideology. Anyone who dares to speak the truth in the 'New Ireland' will be seen as a subversive - an enemy of the state. 'Liberal' governments know how to stifle debate and suppress dissent. Those who expose the hollow rhetoric of liberalism will be denounced as Nazis and fascists. And in due course, they will be charged with hate speech and sent to the Gulag. It happens in Russia, China, North Korea, Saudi Arabia and Iran. It has been reported that the new Irish Justice Minister is planning to introduce 'hate speech' legislation.[9] However, there is a big difference between the vile personal hate speech that 'keyboard warriors' engage in, and the political hate speech that governments engage in. Political hate speech is speech that liberal governments hate hearing. It is a political weapon. It does not apply to blasphemy, which was legalised by the previous Justice Minister. In the 'New Ireland', human killing is legal. Blasphemy is legal. Fake news is legal but telling the truth about the government's abuse of power is regarded as subversive.

Other writers have detailed the abuse of power in the 'New Ireland', for instance John Waters (2018: 46-52)[10]. Liberals in the ruling coalition seem oblivious to the abuse of power by their comrades in government. They do not listen to whistle-blowers who dare to make protected disclosures over such matters as white-collar crime, economic fraud and scams, medical negligence by the State, environmental pollution by semi-state bodies, illegal mortgage charges by banks and building societies, work safety issues, extortionate rent increases by landlords, the location of wind farms and electricity pylons, the destruction of urban villages in order to create bus corridors and the depopulation of rural Ireland. Whistle-blowers are forced to take legal action. All they ever get from the government is the promise of an investigation which will go on endlessly over several years with no end in sight, costing millions of euro. The person seeking redress will suffer terribly. The liberal state will simply put them through hell. We are now living in a state bedevilled by secrecy, corruption, intimidation and character assassination. I speak as an alien in the 'New Ireland'. I cannot close my eyes to the madness that is the new normal here. I do not wish to live in a state where democracy, equality, respect for life and justice are token words. In 1916, James Joyce said: 'Ireland is the old sow that eats her farrow.'[11]

My essays express my profound grief at the demise of the republic founded in 1921 following the War of Independence. Our current 'liberal' government, driven by secularism, uses unethical procedures to persuade the public to approve of its toxic ideology. Aided and abetted by the 'liberal' media, its inner circle excels at propaganda, brainwashing, and misinformation. The ruling elite has legalised such abominations as human killing, sexual aberration, blasphemy and economic inequality. These are the new norms of the 'New Ireland.'

Clearly, we live in a changing world and we need to understand how change should be managed, what limits should not be transgressed and what values should be preserved. My essays spell out the decline and fall of the Irish Republic. However, a true republic can be restored if the silent majority wake up to the reality of secular humanism and take back the country from the one-eyed cyclops. My advice to every reader is to hold on. Hold on to the word of God as revealed in the Bible. Hold on to your Christian heritage and common decency. Hold on to your Celtic spirituality and goodness. Follow the good advice of the prophet Jeremiah 6:16.

> Stand at the crossroads and look;
> ask for the ancient paths,
> ask where the good way is and walk in it,
> and you will find rest for your souls.

Endnotes:

1   Lise Hand. 'Pope's missionaries are spoiling for a fight. The Times, 2.10.2017, p.19

2   Fionnán Sheahan in the Irish Independent, 3.10.2020, p.12.

3   In August 2020, a Supreme Court judge, Seamus Woulfe, as well as 80 prominent government figures, attended an Oireachtas Golf Society dinner in Co. Galway in breach of COVID-19 restrictions. The so-called 'Golfgate' scandal was seen as one law for the old boy network and another law for ordinary people.

4   gombeenism: In Hiberno-English, originally money lending; now a term for corrupt government, shady politicians and 'who-you- know' politics.

5   Immanuel Jakobovits, Jewish Chief Rabbi of Ireland and the UK has stated that 'Killing children before birth is comparable to the Holocaust'.

6   Václav Havel (1978). 'The Power of the Powerless.'

7   'God's mill grinds slow but sure.' (George Herbert, 1640)

8   Karl Ove Kaausgaard (2021). 'In the Land of the Cyclops'. London: Harvill Secker.

9   Ian O'Doherty, in Review p.24. Irish Independent, 02.01.2021.

10   John Waters (2018). 'Give us back the Bad Roads'. Dublin: Currach Press

11   James Joyce (1916). 'Portrait of the Artist as a Young Man.' Chapter 5

REFERENCES AND FURTHER READING

Blanchard, John (1987). *Ultimate Questions*. Darlington: Evangelical Press

Bourke, James M. (2019). *Reflections on the Abortion Issue in Ireland*. Athy: Lumen Fidei Press.

Brooke, Christopher (2017) (Ed.) *Thomas Hobbes: Leviathan*. London: Penguin Classics

Burke, Edmund (1790). *Reflections on the Revolution in France*. Modern UK edition (1987) by J.G.A. Pocock. Indianapolis: Hackett Publishing Co.

Cicero. *De Re Publica*, Book 3, (54 – 51 BC) and De Legibus, Book 3. See Clinton Walker Keyes (1988). '*De Re Publica; De Legibus*'. (Text in Latin and English). Harvard University Press.

Chomsky, Noam (2017). *Requiem for the American Dream*. New York: Seven Stories Press

Dawkins, Richard. *The God Delusion* (2006). London: Black Swan

Dawkins, Richard (2020), *Outgrowing God: A Beginner's Guide*. London: Black Swan de Burca, Padraig & John F. Boyle (2015). *Free State or Republic?* Dublin: UCD Press

Deneen, Patrick J. (2018). *Why Liberalism Failed.* Yale University Press.

Douay-Rheims Bible. Rockford, IL Tan Books & Publishers.

Eatwell, R. & Goodwin, M. (2018). *National Populism: The Revolt Against Liberal Democracy.*UK: Pelican Books.

Flew Antony (2008). *There is a God.* London: HarperCollins

Grayling, A. C. (2017). *Democracy and its Crisis.* London: Oneworld Publications

Harari, Yuval, N. (2015). *Sapiens: A Brief History of Humankind.* London: Vintage

Hitchens, Christopher (2009). *God is not Great: How religions poisons everything.* New York: Twelve Books

Hutchinson Edgar, David. (2003). *Treasures of the Word: An Introduction to Biblical Manuscripts in the Chester Beatty Library.* Dublin: TownHouse

Johnson, Abby (2014). *Unplanned.* Carol Stream, IL: Tyndale House Publications

Johnson, Abby (2016). *The Walls are Talking.* San Francisco, CA: Ignatius Press

Lennox, John (2019). *Can science explain everything?* Epsom: The Good Book Company

McGrath, Alister (2020). *Through a Glass Darkly: Journeys through Science, Faith & Doubt.* London: Hodder & Stoughton.

McGrath, Alister & McGrath, Joanna C. (2010). *The Dawkins Delusion? Atheist Fundamentalism and the Denial of the Divine.* London: IVP Books

Morgan, Piers (2020). *Wake Up: Why the world has gone nuts.* London: HarperCollins

Neuhaus, Richard John (1986). *The Naked Public Square: Religion and Democracy in America.*

Newman, J. Henry (2014). (Reprint). *The Idea of a University.* Worcester MA: Assumption Press

Norman, Jesse (2014). *EDMUND BURKE.* London: William Collins

Orwell, George (2017). *Orwell on Truth.* London: Harvill Secker

O'Dowd, Niall (2020). *A New Ireland: How Europe's most Conservative country became its most Liberal.* New York: Shyhorse Publishing

O'Neill, Luke (2018). *Humanology: A Scientific Guide to our Amazing Existence.* Dublin: Gill Books.

O'Toole, Fintan (2010). *Ship of Fools: How Stupidity and Corruption sank the Celtic Tiger.* London: Faber & Faber

O'Toole, Fintan (2012). *UP THE REPUBLIC!: Towards a New Ireland.* London: Faber & Faber

Peterson, Jordan (2018). *12 Rules for Life: An Antidote to Chaos.* USA: Penguin Random House.

Piketty, Thomas (2015). *The Economics of Inequality*. Cambridge, MA: Harvard University Press

Quinn, David (2017). *How we killed God*. Dublin: Currach Press.

Rudd, Niall (2008). *Cicero: The Republic and The Laws*. Oxford: Oxford University Press

Thompson, Mel (2003). *Philosophy of Science*. London: Teach Yourself Books

van Maren. Jonathon (2020). *Patriots: The Untold Story of Ireland's Pro-Life Movement*. Life Cycle Books